LOVE & LIGHT BLOOD & BONE

Magick for Witches Who Live in the Real World

Eli Ro

D1736390

The information presented is the author's opinion and does not constitute any health or medical advice. The content of this book is for informational and entertainment purposes only and is not intended to diagnose, treat, cure, or prevent any condition or disease. Please seek advice from your healthcare provider for your personal health concerns prior to taking advice from this book.

For Spence, who helps me fly

FOREWORD

Witchcraft is for the people. Its purpose is to give power to the powerless, to the marginalized, to the voiceless.

Or at least, I've always thought so.

Although it operates necessarily on the fringes and in the shadows, witchcraft shouldn't be needlessly overcomplicated, vague, or expensive.

Or at least, I've always thought so.

So when, in the midst of a global lockdown, I decided to start a witchcraft podcast, I vowed that I would never hide information behind a paywall. There would be no exclusive content for paid subscribers. Anything I had to say, I would say to everyone who clicked play.

Make no mistake, I don't hold judgment for witches who do things differently; we've all got bills to pay, and we've all spent years and even decades accumulating the information we disseminate. But it was important to me to help witches, especially witches who are new to the path, feel empowered. I never want a witch to feel as though there is any magick they can't perform simply because they can't afford to.

Witchcraft is for the people. All the people. So my podcast has no tiers or premium subscriptions, and it never will. It was true from the very first episode and it remains true to this day. And my purpose hasn't changed with the publication of this book. In fact, all of the information contained herein is already available, absolutely free, on my Middle-Aged Witch Podcast.

What I hope to accomplish with this book is not to sell a hundred million copies, but to compile the information from the podcast into an easy-to-follow format with a table of contents and an index, and to transform the episodic nature of a podcast into something more organized for witches who prefer the printed word. If it ultimately helps me to afford a better microphone for the show, then I'll certainly consider it worth my time.

If you're already a listener, I am humbled and grateful to you for helping to support me in this mission. If you're a new friend, then I am excited to get started. We've got so much to talk about.

-Eli Ro

CONTENTS

HERBS & PLANT MAGICK

What specific images does the word 'Witch' conjure? For many of us, the quintessential ideal is the mysterious recluse who lives down the lane. Wild hair tangled with leaves, dirt under fingernails, pockets full of toadstools, a basket of herbs from the garden.

Witchcraft is inextricably tied to such ideas. There is an assumption, and rightly so, that a witch has a general knowledge of common herbs and plants. That a witch knows exactly the right combination to concoct a blend for any need that may arise. An unexpected bill, a wayward lover, the loss of a job, an unkind mother-in-law. The witch knows just what plants will combine to create the perfect spell for the job, and also knows just where to find them.

Becoming such a witch may seem like an enormous undertaking, but the fact is, we've all gotta start somewhere. And it's actually really fun to start learning about the different kinds of plants, herbs, flowers, and trees that are found in your region (and in your local grocery store), and to begin learning how to utilize them in your craft.

Herbs and herbalism are woven so tightly into the fabric of witchcraft, for me at least, that it's almost impossible to separate them, and I want to talk about them in depth and explore what they can offer us in terms of expanding and enhancing the kind of magick we are able to perform..

In magic, herbs offer support and magnification of our spellwork. By researching the herbs and plants that correspond with our intention, or what it is we are trying to manifest, we can amplify our workings by using herbs in all kinds of ways.

We can burn them as incense, steep them in water and drink them as teas, put them in recipes that we are making with magickal intent. We can add them to mojo bags or spell jars, dress candles with them, we can use them to cast circles (especially when working outside; we don't want to use salt and kill the grass), and the list goes on.

But how do we know which herbs to use? It's common to hear these days that rosemary can be substituted for any herb, but it's important to understand why that might be. Rosemary has a lot of magical associations, such as health, love, lust, protection, communication, purification, memory, preventing nightmares, removing negativity, abundance, meditation, loyalty, and fertility. And depending on your source, there are even more properties associated with rosemary. Combine this with the fact that rosemary is inexpensive and easy to come by, and we begin to see why so many people advocate for rosemary as a sort of all-purpose herb.

But this is where I want to make a distinction. We hear a lot in witchcraft circles that intention is everything, and it mostly is, but it also kind of isn't. Intention will get us most of the way there, but we have to also do spellwork that supports the intention. Just throwing any old herb into a spell may not kill its effectiveness, but it may be completely neutral in a working, and worst case scenario, it may actually stunt the potency of the spell a little.

Think about making a cake. If we use salt instead of sugar, we will still get a cake, but it isn't going to be exactly what we want, is it? The end result will still be a baked confection, and we can frost it and decorate it and it may look fine, and it will technically be edible, but no one is going to want to eat it and it isn't going to have the desired effect.

It's the same with spellwork; we can throw things together haphazardly and it's still a spell, but if we just use a little care, we can craft a spell using herbs that will enhance it.

I speak a lot about using ingredients in your workings that speak to you, and that's also another distinction I want to draw. Just because you use something in a spell that doesn't necessarily have the universal properties associated with the intention you're trying to manifest, doesn't mean it won't work as long as the ingredient has meaning FOR YOU.

So as an example, if you're doing a spell to rekindle the flame between yourself and a long-term partner, you may use the traditional love spell ingredients like cinnamon and rose, but you may also use an ingredient that is specific to your relationship. If you and your beloved met at a coffee shop, and it's meaningful to your relationship, you might throw a couple coffee beans from your special shop into the spell just to personalize it.

But other than that, whenever possible, try to use ingredients that correspond with your desired outcome. Now, when you come across a spell that asks for exotic ingredients, expensive ingredients, or ingredients whose use doesn't make sense to you, well this is where the idea of 'intention is everything' can come into play.

If you're using a spell that you found in a book or online, don't immediately jump on Etsy and start adding expensive herbs to your cart. Find out what the herbs in the spell are for so that you can look for suitable substitutions.

There should be very little work you can't do with just the herbs in your kitchen cupboard or found in nature. When a spell calls for black salt, make your own! Use 1 part sea salt, 1 part crushed, charred embers from a fire pit or a fireplace, and add the ashes of all your old incense and burnt spells. Crush them all together with a mortar and pestle, and there you have it. Custom black salt for all your black salt needs, for the low, low cost of zero dollars.

Black Salt

Combine 1 part sea salt, 1 part crushed embers, and 1 part ashes from burnt spells and incense in a mortar. Crush the ingredients together with a pestle, and save in a jar to use as needed.

Generally, when creating any sort of magickal concoction, we want to charge the ingredients and imbue them with our intention. But there are a few exceptions that I have to this rule, and black salt is one of them. This is because I like to make a big batch all at once, but then use it for different purposes. I think of it like any other ingredient in my apothecary, such as basil or rose petals. I keep it ready-made in a jar on my shelf, and I don't charge it until I need it.

What follows here is a short list of common and useful herbs that are going to be invaluable to you as a witch, and as a human being who enjoys food flavored with herbs and spices.

Bay **Laurel:** The first herb I like to recommend for the witch's apothecary is bay laurel, also known as bay leaves. Now, you can buy these in the spice aisle at your grocery store, but they can be a little pricey. However, if you go over to the aisle where the ethnic foods are sold (and oh my gods, do not get me started on the practice of delineating ethnic foods vs. just food) you will often find cellophane bags of spices that are exactly the same as the more expensive jarred herbs, but at a fraction of the cost.

Bay leaves are wonderful for writing manifestations on and then burning them, or they can be crushed and used to dress a candle, or added to a spell jar, or whatever your spell may call for. Bay laurel is used in spellwork for protection, good fortune, success, purification, strength, healing and psychic powers.

Basil: Basil is another herb that's crucial for a witch, and for a cook. Basil is cheap to buy and easy to grow. It's used magically for abundance, love, exorcism, wealth, sympathy, and protection. Dispels confusion, fears & weakness.

Black **Pepper:** Black pepper, yes, plain old black pepper, is great for banishing, exorcisms, and protection.

Chamomile: Chamomile isn't an herb that has a ton of uses outside of tea and magick, but I'm including it anyway because it is so useful magically, and it's cheap to buy and easy to find in the tea aisle. Use this herb for all magick having to do with love, healing, reducing stress, and of course, any time a good night's rest is called for.

Garlic: Garlic, or even garlic powder and garlic salt in a pinch, it all works. Use garlic in magick that calls for healing, protection, exorcism, repulsion of energy vampires, and purification of people, spaces and objects. Used to invoke Hekate.

Lavender: Lavender is similar to chamomile in that it doesn't have a ton of use outside of magic, and there are a lot of herbs that can be substituted for lavender depending on your intention, but nevertheless because it's so well-known and beloved as a magickal herb, I'm including it here. Its magickal uses include love, protection, healing, sleep, purification, and peace. Supports healing from depression. So if you're so inclined, definitely add it to your arsenal. But your magick will not suffer without it.

Nettle: Nettle is readily available in the tea aisle alongside chamomile, and you'll probably never add it to your food for any reason, but there is nothing that works as well and is as easy to come by for dispelling darkness & fear, strengthening the will, and aiding in the ability to handle emergencies, and nettle is supremely healing. Sprinkle in and around the home to drive off evil & negativity, or put some in a sachet and keep under the bed to keep nightmares and night terrors at bay.

Rosemary: I know we've just sung rosemary's myriad praises, but my Virgo in midheaven placement wouldn't be able to rest if I neglected to add it here in alphabetical order. Rosemary is useful in workings associated with health, love, lust, protection, communication, purification, memory, preventing nightmares, removing negativity, abundance, meditation, loyalty, and fertility.

Thyme: And finally, thyme: Attracts loyalty, affection, and the good opinion of others. Wear a sprig to ward off unbearable grief or provide strength and courage when needed. Burn or hang in the home for banishing, purification, and to attract good health for all occupants. Easy to grow, cheap to buy, and it will make your stews and soups positively transcendent.

So there you have it. A modest, yet powerful group of herbs and spices that will help in just about any magical application that a witch may need, and you can get nearly all of these for very little money at the grocery store or even the dollar store, if that's what fits into your life and your practice. And one final thought about that before we leave this topic.

This book and the information contained herein is meant for every witch, at every stage in his or her or their practice, regardless of their financial circumstance or whether or not they practice openly. So while it would be amazing if we all had the means to pop down to the neighborhood occult shop and purchase organic, locally-sourced spell ingredients in beautiful glass jars and display them in our picture-perfect apothecary cabinets, that just isn't reality for a lot of us.

So I am not here for shaming witches who buy their shit at the Dollar General, or Walmart, or the grocery store. That is not what I'm about.

GARDEN WITCHERY

Now, I know gardening is not everyone's bag, some people could not care less about gardening. And I know that some of us who would like to garden may not have an outdoor space for it, maybe we're in an apartment. Or we don't own the home we live in so we can't go digging up the yard. All of that is valid and I understand and I get it.

But we are gonna press on anyway because there are a lot of ways to perform garden magick that won't wreck your manicure if you're not into that, and that don't require five acres of waterfront property if you don't have it. But we can still get all the benefits of that robust earth magic, the grounding properties, the mental and emotional healing that it can provide, and if all that wasn't enough, garden magick is a great way to cultivate relationships with nature deities and nature spirits and build a little sweet, sweet, nature karma.

So what is garden magick and what do I mean by it? Garden magic, to me, is just magick that works with and/or serves nature in a close-to-home sort of way. This might be work that benefits the ecosystem in your own yard or your own home, this includes work that serves the animal population right in your own property or your own neighborhood.

This also includes work that channels the natural energies around you to a designated magical purpose, or it can be as simple as planting specific herbs and flowers that will encourage specific results.

So let's talk about plants to grow in and around your home for the specific purpose of having a witch's garden. I won't talk about lavender or chamomile again, except to say that they are so easy to grow and they will come back year over year, so they're one of those plants that you really only have to buy once. But there's so much more we can grow.

You can weave a strong spell of protection over your house, your apartment, even just your own bedroom using nothing but plants, flowers, and herbs that are considered ornamental by non-witches.

And as an added benefit, if you can put any of these outside, even just on a balcony if you're in an apartment, these plants attract beneficial pollinators like bees, butterflies, and hummingbirds, and the goddess loves that.

Anemones: Anemones are an ornamental flower that is really beautiful and also promotes health and healing. The cool thing about anemones is that they're so beautiful and when you grow them yourself, you'll always have them when you need them for healing spells and rituals.

Gardenia: These are gorgeous flowers and they actually attract benevolent spirits during rituals. Peonies (moreo on that in a moment) work the other way; they repel negative spirits and entities. So you could actually go for the peony/gardenia combo to keep the bad guys away and the good guys nearby.

Geranium: Another great flower for the witch's garden is the geranium. Now, I know I'm in the minority here because I don't really care for the way they smell, but I have geraniums anyway because they promote love and good health, AND they are also used in fertility rites.

I'm not using mine in this way, there will be no more babies forthcoming, thankyouverymuch. But if you're interested in performing fertility magick, geraniums may help.

Honeysuckle: Honeysuckle is one of my all-time favorite shrubs. The smell of my childhood, truly. Now this isn't one that can really be grown indoors, but I felt like it should be included because you never hear about it much in witchcraft, but it's so powerful. Honeysuckle enhances psychic ability and it's also used for money spells. This is one you will want on your property in some way, shape, or form. And of course, nothing smells as good as honeysuckle.

And for the record, jasmine smells amazing too and is also used for money magic. So it's a solid alternative to honeysuckle if that's what you prefer.

Ivy: Ivy is another protective plant. It can be used readily to bind people from doing evil. But it's just very protective in general, and this is one that can obviously be grown outdoors, but is also found in pots of miniature English ivy that grows well in the home.

This category includes Devil's Ivy, also called pothos, which grows inside with almost no effort and is such a commonplace houseplant that no one gives it a second glance. And I feel compelled to mention that devil's ivy is really invasive, so please don't plant it outside.

Marigolds: And the last one I'll mention is the marigold. Marigolds are another protective plant, and they're actually also good in the garden for protecting other plants against pests and this is cool because then you don't have to rely on chemical pesticides which I try to avoid because they're so harmful to the beneficial insect population.

But even better than that, marigolds promote prophetic dreams and psychic ability and, of all things, are known to be helpful in legal matters.

Peonies: Peonies are another flower that you can keep in your garden and no one thinks twice about it. They're inexpensive to buy at the nursery to plant in your flower beds or in a pot in a sunny room, and as we mentioned above, what's so interesting about peonies is that they've been used historically for protection specifically against evil spirits. They've even been used in exorcism rites in some cultures.

So if you feel as though you have a particularly negative spiritual attachment, consider keeping peonies. And if you don't, well it's a good defensive flower anyway.

Roses: Another plant that can be kept inside or outside the home are roses. This seems obvious, I know, but roses are dual-purpose witches' allies. They invite and promote love, luck, and divination abilities, and their thorns are excellent at repelling negativity, especially evil eye or any negativity being aimed in your direction.

Now, there are those mini-rose bushes that frequently come in small pots and those are perfect for apartment witches or those who share a home with disapproving non-witches. And of course large rose bushes, and especially climbing roses are brilliant for catching and redirecting malevolence and negativity.

Violets: The final plant on my little list here is violets. I'm choosing violets because they are perfectly content in containers on a window sill and they just look like happy little potted plants to people who don't know how incredibly magically powerful they are.

Violets are first and foremost a flower of protection, so when they're kept near the windows, they act as a ward keeping negative energies and entities at bay. They also promote peace and they invite luck.

So, if you are interested in starting your witches' garden either indoors or outdoors, or if you're just looking to add a few new plants, consider some of these. They're so beneficial and they just look like beautiful plants and flowers. So if you're not in a position to practice openly, there's nothing overtly witchy about any of these.

←◇→

If you would care to add bird feeders or a bird bath, this is also something that can be a tribute to Gaia, to Demeter, Artemis, Freya, Inanna, Isis, the Morrigan, Rhiannon, Venus, Apollo, Bacchus, Mars, Odin, and Saturn. When done with intention, the simple act of caring for and providing for birds means a lot to so many different deities.

It's a great intentional practice that can turn into a habit and become a regular way to commune with and cultivate a relationship with any of these deities, and also a lot of other entities. Brownies, elves, fairies, and pixies are going to notice and hold you in much higher regard if you're regularly making it a point to serve these animals in this way.

Honoring earth spirits by caring for plants and flowers, by feeding and making your property a safe retreat for birds, by intentionally planting flowers to attract pollinators, all of these acts are building earth magick equity.

Earth magick relates to the 'here and now' in terms of our physical health, our stability, and our financial security. So while we are performing acts of service for nature and the animals in our own local area, we are also calling in that earth magick abundance. It is symbiotic, it is mutually beneficial.

If we can be diligent stewards of all the life forms around us up to and including plants and animals which have their own spirits and their own life forces, we are weaving ourselves into the great tapestry.

←◇→

Spiral gardens, cairns, and garden pentacles are a lot more openly witchcraft-related. But if there's nothing stopping you, these are cool additions to a witch's garden. Spiral gardens are moving more mainstream these days, and you can find a lot of cool results online if you want to see what this looks like.

In witchcraft, spirals symbolize birth, life, death, and regeneration, so they're very powerful symbols. And of course a garden itself represents this every single year beginning in the spring with new life, blossoming into a full, lush garden in the summer, producing fruits and vegetables for the autumn, and finally dying back to rest for the winter.

A cairn is just a pile of stones built as a landmark or to denote some kind of religious significance, and these can be as small or as large as you'd care to make them and you can make just one or several as you see fit. These can be dedicated to a specific deity or an ancestor, or as a tribute to the property itself. You may use several to create and define a liminal space or a ritual area.

The purpose of these cairns is to really be a point of focus for whatever purpose you intend to use them for. And again, there are a lot of reference pictures online that you can use for instruction and inspiration, but the point is they're a fun, interactive form of earth and garden magick you can use in your own practice.

Finally, garden pentacles are just that, they are pentacles demarcated on the earth with stones or paving bricks. You could also make a temporary one using seasonal garden debris like pinecones. I've even seen a really beautiful one made of seashells.

These temporary pentacles are especially interesting because you don't have to devote a permanent space for something like that, and they can be used in a customized way to coincide with the change of seasons or to coordinate with a sabbat. You could make one using spring flowers for Ostara or fall leaves for Samhain. And then after your ritual or once the sabbat ends, you can just let nature retake those materials.

If you do have the space and the freedom to make a garden pentacle that's more permanent, you can even plant certain herbs or plants in the open spaces of the pentagram. We have one in our backyard that we made using river rocks, and I've planted purple and white alyssum in the star for protection and to promote peace, and then in the outer circle we have thyme for health, love, and to promote psychic power.

I would like to have been able to use a wider variety of herbs for ir, but my neighbor has this huge bastard of a willow tree that hangs directly over that space and it never sees the light of day, so I can't really plant anything else because it just doesn't get any sunlight.

And yes I suppose I could move the pentagram somewhere else, but then I'd have this whole area under the canopy of that tree that I can't use for anything else. So we make do with what we have. That's the witch way. And how could I even complain about such a minor issue? I am really fortunate that I can even have a garden pentacle at all. It was a dream of mine for a long time.

KITCHEN WITCHERY

You can go online and find a thousand different explanations and cute little graphics that describe what it means to be a kitchen witch, but for me it really comes down to witchcraft that is borne from the desire to create a peaceful home environment, that seeks to promote a harmonious sort of refuge from the outside world for a witch, in which she or he can create powerful magick or find solace, especially in times of external chaos.

If a witch has a family at home, then that's fine, but if a witch does not, if a witch lives alone or still lives with their parents, or if a witch's family does not support or condone witchcraft, the purpose of kitchen witchery is still the same. The haven that a witch creates can be meant for the witch alone. If a witch has a full time job, works outside the home, lives in a tiny apartment, doesn't have a big, beautiful kitchen, whatever the case may be, kitchen witchery is still there to be drawn upon, to create that calm, comfortable environment.

So how do we use kitchen witchery to create this? Well let me start by extolling the many virtues of my personal favorite method. I have probably sung the praises of tea in nearly every episode. I could probably call it the Middle-Aged Tea Lady Podcast and it would be dead-on balls accurate. But this is simply because tea is such an easy, accessible, AFFORDABLE, and effective form of witchcraft.

Consider it: the very act of making tea is such a ritual. You've got to choose the blend you're going to use, according to your own personal tastes and the properties of the herbs you're trying to take advantage of. Even if it's something as simple as a cup of chamomile before bed. Then, you've got to boil your water, steep your herbs, wait for it to cool a little bit, and then drink it carefully and with mindfulness. Stir a little honey into it, clockwise to draw in peace and restfulness, or counterclockwise to banish stress or negativity or whatever you're trying to release.

Bing, bang, boom. Kitchen witchery.

Teas are one of the most common potions that we have access to. And this is a witch activity that we don't need privacy for, we don't have to hide it, we don't have to cast a circle, we don't have to wait for a moon phase, we can do this at any time of the day or night. I keep boxes of different kinds of tea at work. Sometimes, if it's a particularly hellish week, having a cup of tea at my desk saves my sanity. Having favorite teacups or mugs is a total witch thing. These vessels are tools of the craft, just like your cauldron or your altar. And again, it's easy and inexpensive to find a few that you love.

So when life is chaotic, or you feel like things are starting to spiral, or you just really need to press pause on the world and take back a little control, consider tea as a ritual for creating that for yourself.

If you absolutely cannot stand tea, then use coffee, or cocoa, or hot cider. I prefer tea, just because the herbs that I choose can be so powerful and can add so much beyond the pure ritual aspect of it. But this is your craft, and you can practice it in whichever way you damn well please.

Cooking and baking of course will always spring to mind when we talk about kitchen witchcraft, and this is for good reason. The food we eat can be medicine for our bodies, minds, and souls. But this is reality, and we are all very busy. We rarely have the time to make a big meal for ourselves. But we can make small gestures that add up to witchcraft.

Making a pasta sauce from scratch is awesome, but if that's not in your wheelhouse, try stirring some extra basil into your jar of Ragu to draw in wealth. Or adding a little extra ginger to your Panda Express for confidence. Add some extra garlic to your can of chicken soup when you're not feeling well. Its magick will support you in your healing, and frankly it will improve the taste.

We don't have to be Martha Stewart; we just have to consider ways that we can incorporate the craft into our daily lives. And by taking those few extra moments to do these things, we are also practicing mindfulness. We are more easily able to keep our intentions in mind throughout the day.

Baking is a really potent form of witchcraft, and of course baking anything from scratch is an opportunity to create something very magickal. But even when we use shortcuts like box mixes and store bought pie crusts, we can find ways to call in Kitchen Witchery.

If we are using a refrigerated pie crust, we can use a knife to carve intentions, manifestations, even sigils into the bottoms of our pies. We can add extra cinnamon to the apple pie filling for protection. If we're baking a cake from a box, add some vanilla to the mix for love.

Obviously, there are larger and more complicated forms of spellwork that we can (and do!) perform as witches, but in terms of daily acts that we can take to support ourselves in our practices, kitchen witchery is some of the easiest and least labor-intensive. Because all we are doing is adding intention to things that we already have to do each and every day.

Consider simple chores, like cleaning our houses, washing our floors, doing laundry. All of these acts can become witchcraft. Sprinkling a little salt in the rug before vacuuming is a great way to get rid of funky old energy. Adding some rosemary to your Pinesol before you mop or scrub down the kitchen and bathroom will do the same. Creating infused room sprays can serve as a great way to clear out the energetic cobwebs as well.

Infused Room Spray

Put some water in a jar, and add a teaspoon each of any herbs that match up with your purpose, such as lavender for peace and lemon peel for positivity. Cover the jar and charge it overnight in the full moonlight. In the morning, strain out the herbs and pour your infusion into a spray bottle. Spray into the air, onto your carpets or rugs, onto your furniture, even your bedding. Don't soak everything, just give it all a light spritz.

And one last little thing I'd like to mention is keeping a witches' calendar. This is a good, low-effort way to keep track of things like retrogrades, moon cycles, and sabbats. I know that Llewellyn sells one every year, and I know that theirs is not the only one available. But the artwork is always really beautiful, and most of us need a calendar anyway. And just so we're clear, this is not a paid endorsement, I don't personally even have that specific calendar, I just happened to see it the other day when I was at our local occult shop.

And that isn't actually kitchen witchery per se, but it's just kind of an easy way to stay organized in your mundane life as well as your witch life. I am like most of us, I have a lot going on, I always have several balls in the air at any given time, and the only way I get anything done is by writing shit down. Again, these aren't grand magical gestures, these are small, doable methods for bringing extra magick into your daily life.

We aren't witches ONLY during the full moon or on sabbats or during elaborate spells. We are also witches when we're at the grocery store, at work, when we're sick, when we're spending time with family and friends. We are witches 365 a year, 24 hours a day. And kitchen witchery is a really good way to reflect on that and to remember that.

We are so goddamn powerful, even when we're sipping a cup of lemon zinger tea on the couch watching Supernatural reruns. It's not always dark and mysterious; we can't maintain that 100% of the time. And that's why I like to bring in those simple elements of Kitchen Witchery.

FORAGING

Let's talk about foraging. Now, I always try to suggest ways to acquire materials for spellwork that don't require spending money, whenever possible. I think that it helps connect us a little more with the outcomes of our spellwork when we have had to expend the energy to go physically looking for what we need, and it's important to me that the information I give is accessible for witches at every socioeconomic level.

Not every witch has access to an occult shop in their town, and certainly not every witch can afford to spend money on spell materials either in person or online. But mostly, it needs to be remembered that witchcraft is meant to be practiced within a witch's personal means.

A lot of spells we find in books or online will call for ingredients that are expensive or hard to come by, but we don't need to let that be a barrier for doing the kind of work that we want to do.

So before you drive to the witch shop or hop on Etsy, or before you even go to your own grocery store to buy a $15 jar of vanilla beans, let's look to nature to provide what we need. We are all witches, every day, no matter how long we have been practicing, or how long it's been since we performed any kind of magick with deliberation. That is a given. But sometimes it's nice to get a little dirt under our fingernails and really do the act of witchcraft.

So let's get into it. First things first, let's talk about foraging plant materials. Most spells require some kind of plants or herbs, and this is where a lot of witches become a little bit stymied in their desire to perform spells when they can't find the exact plant that a spell calls for. But it is easy as hell to find substitutions, and a lot of them can be found in our literal backyard.

So for this little exercise, I say start close to home and look around at what plants, weeds, shrubs and trees are in your own yard or apartment complex or neighborhood. Obviously, there will be a lot of plants and trees that are easy to identify and that will be very useful to you as a witch.

Pine trees, willow trees, oak, maple, pepper trees, birch, apple trees, and so on are very common, easy to identify, and can be very useful in magic. You are also likely to find flowers, depending on the time of year. Something as simple as rose bushes can be found almost anywhere, and of course the petals, thorns, and even the rosehips are all incredibly magical.

Other flowers that are both powerful magickal allies and common to most areas (of the States at least), are marigolds, zinnias, violets, sunflowers, daisies, peonies, feverfew, chamomile, lavender, poppies, morning glories, and the list goes on. There are very few flowers that don't have some sort of magical correspondence, so go out into your neighborhood and see what's out there.

"But Eli," you say, "I don't know what any of the trees, flowers or plants in my area are, I'm not a botanist."

Fair enough. Neither am I. There is an app that I use called PlantNet that identifies plants for me. It's completely free, and you just take a picture of the unidentified plant you find and the PlantNet app will use its massive database to tell you what exactly it is. You can take pictures of the different parts of the plant, flower, or tree to more accurately narrow down precisely what you're looking at, and it's a really great, completely free resource for foraging close to home.

I recommend you grab a notebook and pen and take a walk. While you're taking pictures and identifying the plants, make a note in your notebook about what the plant is and where you found it, and then when you get back home, you can spend a little time researching what possible magical properties those plants might have. So when you're doing a protection spell that calls for wolf's bane, you'll be able to Google its magickal properties.

Then you can flip through your witch's field guide and discover that you can substitute fern fronds that you got from the park and get the same effect.

And by the way, if there's a field or empty lot near you that's overgrown with weeds, don't overlook what an absolute goldmine it might be for witchcraft materials. Dandelion, nettle, plantain, purslane, clover, thistle and more are all considered invasive pests by gardeners, but are powerful magical and medicinal plant allies.

Here is my disclaimer though, **do not use a plant internally or medicinally if you're not sure whether it's been sprayed with pesticides.** It'll still work perfectly well for spells, but you won't want to make nettle tea with a plant you've found in the park because there's a good chance it's been sprayed with chemicals.

Do this little exercise at different times of year as well, because there will be a lot of plants you don't find in January that you will find in June, and vice versa.

This is a great way to build your own grimoire with locally sourced plants that you have personally discovered and researched, and next time you see a spell that calls for something exotic, you'll be better able to replace it with something free that you've foraged on your own. And let's be honest, we all want to be the neighborhood witch gathering mysterious flora into a basket.

But there's so much more to forage than just plants! Let's go through some commonly foraged materials that we can use in our craft:

Dirt, literal soil, has really formidable magical properties. If you're doing any kind of grounding spell, you're going to want dirt. If you're doing earth magic, get yourself some meadow or forest dirt. If you're doing baneful magic, hexes, or curses, use graveyard dirt. If you're doing wealth and abundance magic, bank dirt. Do you have a legal issue coming up? Use courthouse dirt. To add extra power to any spell you're doing, use crossroads dirt. If there's a spell you're doing to affect someone else, sneak a little soil from their yard.

The only warning I will give here is to be ethical, safe, and respectful. Don't take dirt from anywhere you're not supposed to be, and if you are going to use graveyard dirt, use the grave of a family member when you can, or ask permission from the spirit of the person when you can't. Regardless of where you get the dirt, leave an offering of some kind. In the case of crossroads dirt, the customary offering is 12 pennies, leaving 3 at each corner of the crossroads.

Cobwebs are a little weird as a collector's item, maybe, but bear with me. The next time you come across a big old cobweb, collect it carefully, and stick it in a jar until you need to do a good binding spell. If it's a little too much for you, a little too icky, I get it, but I am telling you if you add spiderwebs to your spell, it will bind somebody good and tight.

Snakeskins aren't something we find every day, but if you're lucky enough to find them out in nature somewhere or if you happen to have a friend with a pet snake, snakeskins are beautiful to use in spells for transformation, or when you want to leave something behind and make a clean start, or anytime you're trying to level up in some way.

Feathers found in nature are a huge, big deal for a lot of witches. We may interpret these as messages from our guides, from departed loved ones, or from the very universe itself. And this can depend on the color of the feather or from which type of bird it came, too. There are a lot of different ways to interpret those things, and you can look online for those correspondences, but you can actually take it upon yourself to determine what sort of message a particular feather may be, as well.

Not everything in witchcraft has a hard and fast explanation, especially when it comes to signs and omens, because a lot of factors can come into play. Different cultures and different witchcraft traditions can have completely opposing interpretations for, say a crow feather.

Some cultures revere crows as messengers from the other side, and others believe they are harbingers of death. Even a witch's personal life experiences may dictate that certain feathers or certain birds mean something specific that goes against the grain of common explanations.

So you can kind of write your own story when it comes to feathers. Spend a little time considering what comes to mind when you think of different types of birds that are common to your area. Jot down those impressions in your grimoire.

When you do see feathers in your day-to-day life, consider what you may have had on your mind just at the moment when you found the feather. Were you thinking of a lost loved one, or an old flame, or were you thinking maybe about some issue you've been losing sleep over?

If mourning doves make you think of your granddad, or if you've been struggling with an issue for a while, perhaps this feather is a message that things are going to be okay. If crows have negative connotations in your tradition, and you've been very preoccupied with a toxic relationship, maybe that feather is a sign to get some distance between yourself and this toxic person.

All of this is just a long way to say that feathers are wonderful messages from the universe, but we need to decide how we want to read them. If you have no special associations with birds or feathers at all, then by all means, ask Google what a specific feather means. But when you do find them in nature, forage them, because they can be very useful in magic.

Depending what your personal connotations are, you can use these different feathers to add a lot of power to your personal workings. And there's no getting around the fact that feathers are associated with air magic, so you can definitely use these feathers in your own air magick spellwork.

Bird's nests are a little more rare to find. Sometimes when you're out in nature you will come across an old, abandoned bird's nest. These are great for your spells that may be directed toward home magic. If you're doing a spell to create a more harmonious, calm household or family life, or if you're doing any fertility magic, a bird's nest will be a welcome addition. They can also be really gorgeous on an altar for Ostara or Beltane, since they're associated with fertility.

If you're concerned about any mites or creepy crawlies in the nest, and you frankly should be, there's a simple process for sterilizing it. First, leave it out somewhere dry and sunny for a few days to get rid of any odors. Then stick it in a paper bag and freeze it to kill anything that may be living in it, and finally spray it with Lysol to kill any bacteria.

Wasp or hornet nests are perfect for hexes, protection magic, and banishings. Just please for the love of god make sure they're old abandoned nests and are not currently in use. Use the same process as we did with bird's nests for sterilizing them so you're not introducing anything funky into your house, and then use them as you see fit.

Broken glass is always helpful to keep on hand for curses. When I find bits of broken glass, I put them in a jar in my cupboard for those rare occasions when I need to make a spell jar, a witch bottle, or something that calls for broken glass. Obviously, please be very careful when you're foraging things like glass, nails and thorns, and do wear gloves or at least carry a pair when you go out foraging.

Broken mirrors are excellent additions to spells for deflection of negativity, if you feel like someone has been thinking daggers in your direction, a deflection spell will help to turn their evil eye back on themselves and prevent you from getting the worst of it. Broken mirrors are also really good for revenge spells. It's the same principle as deflection, we are turning their own awful actions and behaviors back onto them.

Rusty nails are a key ingredient in witch bottles, but please don't give yourself tetanus. And if you are ever fortunate enough to find **railroad spikes**, snatch them up. If you can find four, holy shit. Iron spikes placed at the entrance of your home, and especially placed at the four corners of your property, are brilliant for protection.

Scraps of clothing or fabric, and I mean your ratty old things, are a great resource. If it's too crappy for the Goodwill pile, use it to make mojo bags and poppets. That isn't exactly foraging, but it's kind of like foraging in your own trash, I guess, rather than throwing something out. And it's one of my favorite methods of witchcraft. Stitching your own poppets or mojo bags is such a powerful way to weave your power into the literal fabric of your spells.

And it doesn't have to look professional; if you're not a skilled seamstress, it does not matter. Like everything in witchcraft, the aesthetics are not important AT ALL, despite what social media would have us believe. The magick is in the work.

Antlers are really cool to find. I don't find them much in my area, but when we go up to the cabin sometimes you can get lucky. Antlers are used in fertility magic, protection magick, battle or warfare magick, and sex magick. Antlers and horns are also a great tribute to add to an altar for any of the horned gods, and of course they can be made into wands, jewelry, or totems.

←◇→

Bones! Alright, this next section is going to be a little in-depth. There are a lot of health and safety concerns to keep in mind when foraging bones, and it's such a multi-faceted process. But is there anything in the world as witchy as having a jar of bones in your apothecary?

In my opinion, bones are one of the most fun things to find and forage for your craft. If you find bones that are already picked clean by scavengers and bleached by the sun, lucky you. You still need to disinfect them before handling them with your bare hands though, and for that I recommend 3% hydrogen peroxide. It's basically just what you find at the drugstore that your mom used to pour on your skinned knees.

Cover the bones with hydrogen peroxide and let them sit in a plastic tub (that you don't ever use for any other purpose) for a few hours, then you can scrub them with a brush (again, that you don't use for any other purpose) to get any remaining gristle or connective tissue off them.

Then just cover them in borax or sea salt for 4 to 6 weeks to dry them out. Replace the salt or borax once a week or so. This will make them safe to handle, and from there you can use them to make jewelry, or altar decorations, or of course to use in your spells.

If you find bones that aren't picked clean and bleached by the sun, meaning, you've basically found a carcass, you can leave it where it is and let nature continue to do the work for you while you check up on it every couple weeks.

The downside to this method is that your precious bones may be scattered or carried away by scavengers during this time. If you really want those bones though, you can gather them, using gloves, please, for the love of god, and bury them on your property to let nature do the job in a more controlled environment.

Depending on the size of the animal and the degree to which it's already decomposed, this could take 2-6 months. So it isn't a step to be taken lightly. Bury it two or three feet deep and mark it so you don't lose track of it. If you have a dog who likes to dig, put something heavy on top of it, like a big paving stone. Once it's down to mostly bones, dig it up again and proceed with soaking your carcass in water and powdered laundry detergent that has enzymes. I like regular old powdered Tide.

Make sure your detergent has enzymes in it! This breaks down connective tissue. Change the water and detergent every week or so and wear gloves. The word of the day is gloves. This step may take two weeks, it may take eight. It just depends. Once this step is over, proceed with the hydrogen peroxide step and then the salt/borax step. This kind of witchcraft is time consuming and not really something you see on Tiktok. But it's real.

And bones in witchcraft are really powerful tools. They're used for protection, as tributes, and depending on the animal the bones are from, they are invaluable as materials for spellwork. Bird bones are good for abundance and fertility and magic, coyote bones are good for shamanic and transformation magic, and so on.

Figure out what animal you're working with and research the ways you can use the gift of bones you've received. If you can't figure out what kind of bone you've got, you can still use it for general protection magic, or as a totem, or in jewelry, or really however you like.

SPELLWORK

O kay, enough foreplay. We all know that one of the coolest things about being a witch is creating and performing spells. This is our time to really shine, when the rubber meets the road, and we find ourselves bent over a bubbling cauldron (or a Crockpot, as it were), stirring an undulating concoction made of mysterious and dangerous ingredients lit only by the pale, silvery light of the full moon.

So let's spend a little time talking about what makes a spell, as well as how best to create our own spells (or at least customize other witches' spells for our own use).

What is a spell, exactly? Well, a spell, to my mind, is simply combining intention with action to create a desired outcome. This does not always mean some big grand gesture, and I think that's where spellwork can kind of be intimidating for a lot of newer witches, and even some not-so-new witches. There are a lot of small gestures we all do that qualify as spells under my definition.

Making a birthday wish is probably the spell we're all most familiar with, and it's probably the first spell many of us ever performed. Someone prepares the cake and lights the candles, everyone sings the ritual chant, you make the wish, and you blow out the candles. Boom. Spell.

Recognizing these smaller-scale spells in our daily lives makes it easier to know where to begin crafting larger-scale, more far-reaching and longer-lasting spells. Plus, it's just smart to stay practiced. It's easier to be comfortable and confident in spellmaking when we realize that we are doing it all the time.

Okay cool, so where to begin? Well for starters, identify your intention, and then decide what kind of spell you're going to cast. By this, I mean are you going to craft a spell jar? A mojo bag? Maybe a sigil or a ritual candle? Some people are very particular to a type of spell medium. One of my daughters is very partial to sigils, my other daughter is very partial to mojo bags.

I personally do a lot of candle magic. I also like potions, usually in the form of teas that I mix to my own specifications and for my own purposes. So consider that too. If you're going to do a spell, there's nothing wrong at all with revisiting the same kind of spellwork over and over again if it's something that you're comfortable with.

Next, I suggest that a witch thinks about what speaks to them when considering their intention. Before you do a Google search or consult Llewellyn's Complete Book of Correspondences, ask yourself what comes to your own mind when you think about your intention.

For example, a spell for connecting with ancestors makes me think of passionflowers and peppermint, due to my grandmother always having passionflowers and peppermint in her garden. It isn't an obvious connection and it won't be found in Cunningham's Herbal Encyclopedia, but it is a personal connection for me, and therefore will be a strong addition to my spellmaking.

Always consider what is personally meaningful to you when you are in the planning and development stages of your spell. Consider a witch who may be working a spell for health and wellness. Perhaps this hypothetical witch's mother used to make Campbell's chicken soup when she was sick, and this witch now associates it with feeling better. This witch might consider crushing some chicken bouillon into her spell jar, or rubbing it onto her candle.

Whatever it is that you associate most strongly with your intention is where you should begin when crafting your spell.

Once you've exhausted the depths of your own imagination, then move toward other resources for correspondences.

An important note for trying to reproduce spells that you find online or in books: more than almost any other consideration, it is important to understand WHY a spell may call for certain ingredients. If you are trying to work an abundance spell and you find a cool spell online, make sure that you understand the purpose of each ingredient, because then you can substitute and alter a spell to your specifications, needs, and to the ingredients that you have at your own disposal.

If a spell calls for something like Irish Moss, I'm going to have a hard time finding that. And so will any witch living in southern California. But if we know that one of the properties of Irish Moss is to give good luck, then we can look for some other herb or plant that carries the same properties that's easier to find. So in this example I would probably go with nutmeg or orange peel, because they're also associated with good luck, and they're a lot easier for me to get a hold of.

So, the moral of that story is, understand why you're being asked to use certain ingredients, and you'll be better able to find suitable substitutions without having to spend a lot of money, or go out of your way to attain them.

Speaking of, where should a witch begin looking for ingredients? Well, we do love an aesthetic spell, but social media has made so many of us feel insecure about our practices because our altars aren't constructed of artfully dried flower arrangements and vintage glass spell jars and leather bound grimoires.

It can be difficult, time consuming and expensive to try and replicate the so-called witchy aesthetic we see on social media. And sometimes, frankly, it isn't safe for us to be really open with our practice.

So where to go for spellmaking ingredients that aren't going to cost too much, be too difficult to get ahold of, and too obvious as to their intended purpose?

Let's begin with jars and bottles. Obviously, witches have been collecting, repurposing, and saving jars since jars were invented. There is really no need to buy a bunch of jars unless you want to and it's financially feasible for you. Save your pickle jars, your jelly jars, your olive oil jars. Give them a good washing and use them well.

For mojo bags, if that's your thing, I would say they're not too hard to find and they're generally not very pricey at all. You can get wedding favor bags at Michaels, Target, even the dollar store in their little wedding decoration section. They often come in different colors that you can correspond to your intention, or if nothing else, you can just sew them.

As we spoke about in the foraging chapter, cutting up old clothes to create a mojo bag is totally free, and it's very powerful. With each stitch, you are literally creating the vessel to hold your spell. You do not have to be any kind of seamstress to make a simple mojo bag, and it's going to be a lot more powerful than buying a pretty (yet pricey) premade mojo bag online.

But spices! Every witch knows that there's literally no difference between purchasing basil from an apothecary and purchasing basil from the spice aisle at Albertson's. It comes down to what makes the most sense for you. It's also dead easy to grow most household herbs from seeds, and a great way to get started on your kitchen witch path, if that's a path that calls to you.

And on that note, most grocery stores sell common herb seedlings like basil, rosemary, thyme, and mint in little pots in the produce department. They cost a couple dollars each, you can bring them home and repot them, and now not only can you grow herbs for spellmaking, but also for cooking as well.

One caveat for this example, as far as growing herbs from seeds, rosemary is the exception. Rosemary has a really low germination rate, and it's generally not worth one's time to grow from seed, even for an experienced gardener. But it still costs about as much to buy a small rosemary plant as it does to buy a small jar of dried rosemary at the grocery store, and you can always propagate it and have more rosemary.

Basil, sage, dill, oregano, mint, and lavender are easy herbs for even novice gardeners to grow, they look super cute, and they are useful in cooking, tea-making, and witchcraft.

Another great source I have found for spell ingredients is in the tea aisle. Are you sick of hearing about tea yet? A lot of herbs that are trickier to come by can be found in the tea aisle, and they're usually extremely affordable.

Herbs such as nettle, passionflower, echinacea, lemon balm, chamomile, and raspberry leaf are easy to find as teas, and they're so useful. And not only as a tea; if your spell calls for nettle, you can easily tear open a teabag and now you've got your herb.

ELEMENTAL MAGICK

Earth, air, fire and water are the four elements that we witches most often work with, although spirit is the fifth, and certainly the most important. We connect fire with creativity and passion, we connect water with emotions, intuition, and psychic ability, and earth magick is associated with wealth and abundance and overall physical health. Air corresponds with logic, reason, and communication. Let's consider how we might incorporate each of the elements into our magick.

Air Magick: I thought I would start this chapter with Air Magick. I know that air magick is probably the least sexy kind of magick that we do, but I also believe that air magick can really boost all those other kinds of elemental magic. If you're doing a spell to sweeten your relationship with a friend, family member, partner or someone you've got a romantic interest in, then incorporating air magick into that working is going to enhance and strengthen the lines of communication and cooperation with that person.

Further, if you're feeling a lack of creative spark and you want to do some fire magick to breathe some new life into a creative project, air magick can help clear out the mental cobwebs so to speak, and inspire new ways of looking at things. Air can give you more freedom of thought, and uninhibited thinking.

For earthy wealth and abundance spells, consider incorporating air magick to open opportunities for maybe a new job or a promotion, especially something that might include travel.

One of my favorite reasons to use air magick is for ancestor and spirit work. Our ancestors and our spirits exist in an ethereal realm. So it can be helpful, especially if we're having difficulty connecting to them, if we try to meet them on their own turf, so to speak.

Of course, our ancestors and spirit guides are always with us everywhere, and we don't really need to do any special, extravagant workings to speak and commune with them. But if a witch is having trouble making that initial connection, or if we just want to deepen an existing connection, air magick is the way to go.

Air magick is sort of the unsung hero in elemental magick, and I'm not just saying that because I'm a Libra. So now that I've bored you with all the reasons you should be doing more air magick, let's talk about what that means and what it looks like.

Air magick is performed in a lot of different ways. I think that after blowing wishes on dandelions, the most well-known kinds of air magick are incense and smoke cleansing or smudging, if that's part of your practice. Meditation, spell powders, breath work, and wishing papers are also forms of air magic.

So let's break them down:

Incense and smoke cleansing are pretty self-explanatory. Burning incense is used for purification and cleansing. In fact, this is why Catholics use incense during Mass, as well as symbolically representing the prayers of the faithful rising to the heavens. Incense is used by witches to sanctify and cleanse altar tools, spell jars and other vessels, and it can cleanse and clear physical spaces.

Oftentimes, incense can be used to create a circle for spell work. In the event that you can't or don't wish to use salt to cast a circle, incense and smoke can create the same kind of sacred space without having to be vacuumed up later, or without dumping salt on the earth. Which, please, don't do that.

The cool thing about incense is that it comes in about a million different scents and varieties. You can use specific kinds of incense to align with the spell work you're doing as well. For example, if you're doing a money manifestation, you can use a cinnamon incense to give some extra power to the spell, or you can buy a specially made prosperity blend or money drawing incense.

Another one of the great things about incense is that it's easy to find (and it's inexpensive). You can also make your own incense, but this can be dangerous sometimes, and it's not really in the scope of this book. Not every herb is safe to inhale when it's burning.

Which brings me to another important caveat: when you're burning incense, or sage, or palo santo, cedar, rosemary, whatever, always open your windows. Don't burn shit with those windows closed. You're going to give yourself an asthma attack or set off the smoke detectors and don't say I didn't warn you. I promise you, this warning comes from experience.

Meditation and breathwork are also air magick. We all know how important it is to practice meditation and how difficult it can be to quiet our minds and work on visualization or connecting with our guides and ancestors. So practicing meditation can really be useful for those issues, not to mention manifestation and lucid dreaming. And it's all air magick, baby!

Breathwork is of course closely associated with meditation, but it's also a convenient way to cleanse when you're out and about and don't have access to a bowl of salt or a stick of incense. If you're working with tarot and the energy of the deck feels a little stale, try blowing on the cards, or giving the deck a few knocks with your knuckles. It's an air magick way of dusting off any janky energy that's hanging around them.

Spell powders are something that I don't generally see a lot of information about these days. And I think it's a shame, because they're easy to use, they're portable, and they're really effective. A spell powder is basically a powder made of your own special blend of ingredients that you've personally sourced and ground up to use for your own purpose.

Protection Spell Powder

Combine dill, lavender and eggshells in your mortar and pestle or in a spice grinder and make a fine powder. Charge your powder with your energy and intentions, and use it to sprinkle across thresholds and windowsills for protection. This is especially useful when traveling or staying in hotels.

You can make powders for any purpose, and release the powders into your environment or into the air to carry your manifestations out into the world. The cool thing about them is that they're portable and discreet. You can take a spell powder to a body of water (assuming you're not putting anything noxious or toxic in your blend), you can take it to a forest, a park, even a mountain top and release your will into the world at large.

Spell powders allow us to take our magickal workings to all kinds of places where it might be difficult to perform more traditional spellwork.

You can even create a powder for manifesting a job at a place you want to work and then distribute your powder directly at the site. The uses for spell powders go on and on, and I don't think it gets enough attention.

Lastly, I want to talk about wishing papers. These are specially made papers that you can find online or at your favorite occult shop. You simply write your spell, sigil, or desired manifestation on the paper, you roll it into sort of a tube shape, and you light it. Wishing paper doesn't really burn per se, it just sort of smolders.

When the paper finally smolders down to the base, it just floats away and disappears. It's the coolest thing. And you don't have to worry about sparking a wildfire, because wishing papers are meant to be used indoors. I love wishing paper. It's really fun for kids too, to write out their wishes and then watch them float into the ether.

Fire Magick: Next, we'll talk about fire magick, which is much sexier than air magick. Some of the intentions or specific spellwork that sort of falls under the Fire Magick umbrella might be any work that seeks to activate or awaken something. Aggression and anger are fire emotions, so if you're trying to guard against aggression or diffuse or control anger, think fire. Ambition is also ruled by fire, as are confidence and creativity. Those are all very intermingled and intertwined as well.

Desire and destruction, lust, sexual energy and love (although deep and sincere love is also ruled by water), inspiration, leadership, even magick itself is guided by fire. Fire magick entails all of those things you would expect, like candle magick, cauldron magic, lust magick and passion magick. A lot of kitchen magick is ruled by fire as well, especially cooking and baking.

But even if those kinds of magick aren't really your forte, you can still incorporate the element of fire into your magical workings simply by using ingredients that are ruled by the element of fire. It's a way of combining different kinds of magick into something really powerful and cohesive, and that kind of flexibility and experimentation are really quintessentially witchcraft.

I mean, that's the kind of freedom that drew so many of us away from organized religions and dogmatic ways of thinking in the first place.

Say for example, you're someone who really loves spell bottles or creating ritual teas. Or maybe you're just working a spell that you want to be a slow-release kind of working, so rather than burn it, you want to bury it instead.

But maybe because of the specific kind of spell that it is, say a love spell or a creativity spell, you need to also call upon the power of fire. How do we combine a non-fire spell method with those powerful and potent qualities of fire?

Well, in these cases, one way would be to use fire-aligned ingredients. So if we're talking about herbs, flowers, and plants, that would include allspice, basil, bay, tangerine, orange, lime (all of the citruses really), pineapple, clove, rosemary, witch hazel, sunflowers, oak, dragon's blood, fennel, mustard seed, walnut, St. John's wort, chrysanthemum, curry, pepper, horseradish, cinnamon, ginger, chili peppers, frankincense, thistle, pomegranate, and so forth.

But there are other kinds of things as well, like certain minerals and crystals. Topaz, tourmaline, especially red tourmaline, red agate, red calcite, garnet, red jasper, ruby, onyx, fire opal, pyrite, bloodstone, citrine, and tiger's eye. There are a lot of different stones you can work with to bring some fire power to your spells. You can also wear certain metals, too, like brass, gold, steel, and iron.

Do some research and find out what plants and herbs and stones and metals are ruled by fire, and then dig into the specific magical properties of the herbs themselves to see which ones align with your intentions most closely. And yes, this shit is very time consuming, or it can be at least, but isn't that part of the fun and the experience of creating a spell?

There are certainly a lot of spells online that you can do, but I've said it before and I'll say it again: Any work that you personally create is going to be more potent and more specific to your intentions and you're going to feel a lot more intrinsically involved in the creation of your results.

The more of the work that you personally can do, the more your result will be tailored to your specific, desired outcomes. So, while I touched on this just ever so briefly above, I want to kind of expand on the concept of using fire to burn your spell ingredients, or your sigil or what have you, as a means of enacting a quick and powerful start to the spellwork.

Because fire magick can mean different things, and maybe I should have talked about this in the beginning, but here we are anyway. Fire magick can refer to the kinds of spells that correspond with fire, as we've already discussed, such as creativity, lust, or desire.

But it can also refer to literally using the power and the attributes and the characteristics of fire, like a quick, burning start, or an intensity in your work, and it can also be used in spells where a destructive element is desired, like if you're trying to do a cord cutting or a banishing.

So consider those things as well when you're constructing your spell. If I'm trying to create a lust spell to reignite the passion in my long-term relationship, I might use a spell jar filled with fire spices like cinnamon and chilis, or I might do candle magick and dress it with those herbs. So think about the characteristics of the element that you want to use, and then think about the timeline you're trying to create as well. There's a lot you can combine to make the exact spell you want.

And mostly, as I always say, and as I'm always going to say, just do the goddamn work. Try some shit. It isn't all going to work, and it isn't all going to work the way that you want it to, at least probably not at first.

And that's why it's so important to write things down. Keep track of exactly what work you do, the ingredients you use, the method of spell, the day of the month, the day of the week, the moon phase. And then go back later and update it with your results so that you can keep track of what worked and what didn't, and how long it took. Write down things you want to do differently next time, or write down things you definitely want to keep the same. That way you can codify your own original spellwork.

Do this even if you decide to use someone else's spell from a book or online. It's like a recipe: write down exactly what you did, what you did differently, and what you want to try to do next time. People really underestimate the amount of research and development that goes into witchcraft. It's not just decorating your altar for the seasons and taking pics for social media.

It's very academic in a lot of ways. And I think we should give witches some credit for doing the work and trying to learn as much as they can and for all the trial and error that goes into it. So if you're a seasoned witch or if you've just started along this path, I want to commend you for taking the bold step of forging your own way in this weird world. Make it your own.

We only get one chance at this lifetime, so do the scary thing. Do the original thing. Do what feels most authentic.

Water Magick: Water Magick is always a fun topic, because it's such a vast topic. Water is associated with emotion, relationships, and intuition and psychic ability, and there are about a hundred million subtopics that sort of branch off of those main ideas. And from those branches, you get a hundred million other sub-sub topics. Because when we think of water, we have to remember that it is always in flux.

Water is never fixed, there are still ponds and deep lakes, and there are flowing streams and crashing rivers, and even broad seas and stormy ocean. Although they are all composed of water, they are so completely different as to be classified as completely different environments, and are home to completely different species.

So consider the simple emotion of regret. A pond of regret might be hitting the snooze button one too many times and being late to work. A lake of regret might be passing on a job that could have turned into a lucrative career. A stream of regret might be losing touch with a dear friend, and a river might be the regret of taking a lover for granted and losing them forever.

All of these stem from the same root, and they are all ruled by water, but I think that none of us would equate being ten minutes late to work with losing the love of our lives due to our own mistakes.

But this is why water magick is so special. It can be very shallow, or supremely deep. And I am here for it, so let's dive in. When we think of water magick, a lot of times our minds go straight to moon water. And rightly so; moon water has been a time-tested form of water magick for generations of witches, and I know it's one of the favorite forms of water magick in my family, specifically because it's cheap, easy and effective.

Moon Water

Get a clean glass jar or a bottle. Cleanse your vessel using smoke, incense, or salt, and fill it with purified or filtered water. Then set your intention for this water. Ask yourself, and then answer, what do I hope to accomplish with this water? Imbue this water with that energy. You can even label the jar with your intention. For added power, you may choose to put a water-safe crystal in the water.

Cover your water loosely, and leave it outside during the moon phase that corresponds with your goal. If your crystal is not water-safe, you can always just put it next to or on top of the jar. In the morning, retrieve your jar of water and use it according to your desired outcome.

So now you've got your water, what do you do with it? Well it depends, if you're trying to make more money or increase some kind of talent that you use your hands for, like writing or art, you might want to wash your hands with it a few times a day until it's gone.

You can wash your face or your hair with it if you're doing glamour magick. You can place it on your altar as an offering if you're doing any kind of deity or ancestor work.

You can also drink it. You can use it to make ritual teas by heating it up and steeping your specially selected herbs in it. Use it to water your plants, especially if you're growing any herbs that you intend to use in your future spellwork.

You can use it in any way that you like, whatever will support your own intentions. I will sometimes mix moon water with ashes and black salt to make a paste, and then draw sigils with it. The limit exists only in your imagination. So go nuts.

Now before we move on, I want to talk about crystals, gems, and metals that are NOT safe to mix with water. Obviously, many metals will corrode and rust in water, so unless you're certain that it's pure gold or stainless steel, I don't recommend submerging it.

Minerals and crystals that are common but NOT safe to put in water are: just about any stone whose name ends in ITE, like selenite, malachite, apatite, pyrite, etc. These are generally not water safe, and in fact can become very corrosive and contain heavy metals and carcinogens that are bad for you. Just stay on the safe side and keep them dry.

Opal, black tourmaline, turquoise, gypsum, lapis lazuli, ruby, and moonstone are a few other stones that are very popular, but have no business in water.

With that behind us, let's talk about another favorite form of water magick: the ritual bath or shower. A ritual or ceremonial bath can be as simple or as elaborate as you would like it to be, depending on exactly what it is that you're trying to get out of it.

For a simple, indulgent, self-care sort of bath, the ritual can be as simple as lighting a few scented candles, turning down the lights, pouring some gentle oils into the water, and maybe placing a water-safe crystal in the water with you, such as an amethyst or a rose quartz.

When I say to use oils, please, for the love of the gods, make sure that it will not irritate your skin. Just because it says essential oil on the bottle doesn't mean it'll be safe in your bath, especially in and around your genitals. Cinnamon oil is lovely for dressing candles, but it will give you a scorching UTI if you dump it in your bath water.

Now for a more intentional bath, you'll want to start adding herbs to your water, and you'll also want to maybe consider the moon phase as well to align with your desired outcome (more on moon phases in the Moon Magick chapter). You can even draw a sigil for your intention, which you can paint onto your own body with some kind of skin-safe bath oil with relevant magical properties.

Stress Reducing Ritual Bath Blend

To address emotional or spiritual stress or oppression, or stagnant, undesirable energy hanging over you, combine the following ingredients and charge them with intention: cedar for courage, rosemary for healing, hex-breaking, and personal power, rose petals for peace, lavender , tobacco, and clove for purification.

Obviously, you don't want to just whip a handful of loose herbs into the bathwater unless you just really enjoy backing up your plumbing. So I suggest putting your herbs into some cheesecloth or a muslin bag, or if you're on a budget or just don't want to make a run to the store, you can absolutely use a cotton sock. Tie up the open end and drop it in the tub like a teabag and let it steep.

And speaking of tea (yes, again), you may recall that we talked about inexpensive sources for different herbs, and I mentioned that herbal teas are cheap and easy to find and they have a lot of applications for spellwork. So drop a few bags of nettle tea in the water as well, for protection, purification and healing while you're at it.

Dress, carve, and light some candles. Get into the bath, and just soak. Envision your end goals, really see the end result that you want to achieve from this bath. Whisper a mantra or a spell, over and over again until you really internalize the words. Whatever the intention of your bath is, do the research, gather your ingredients, and carve out some time for your bath.

Now, not every home has a bathtub. And it's also not always practical to take up the bathroom for an hour or so when you share your home with other people. So in those circumstances, I recommend the ritual shower. The preparation is similar. You're going to figure out what you need for your spell and gather those items together, you'll write your spell, mantra, or sigil, and you're going to figure out when is the most opportune time for the work.

But instead of putting the herbs in the bathwater, I suggest steeping all your herbs together in a good size bowl or jar for a good half hour or so, and you can also drop a water-safe crystal in with them, and then strain the herbs out and just keep that water. That is what you're going to use in the shower.

Light your dressed and carved candles, run your shower water, and then carefully wash yourself with the herbal elixir that you've made. Pour it over your skin, pour it over your hair. Speak your spell, do your vision work, make it nice.

You can also do these ritual water ceremonies in natural bodies of water, if you're fortunate enough to live near a pond, lake, river, or sea. Make sure, as always, that none of your spell ingredients are harmful to the wildlife that lives in that body of water, of course, but using a natural body of water for your spell work is a great way to invoke the spirits of that body of water to assist with your intention.

And if that is something that you decide to do, leave an offering when you go. Some rose petals, a few sprigs of fresh rosemary, or if you're going to a lake specifically, you can toss a spoon full of brewer's yeast or good quality corn meal to feed the fish there. Make sure if you do that, you don't do it overly often. It's a treat, and it won't harm the habitat, but be sparing and judicious in your use of it.

Water spirits love the attention, so if you're respectful and you approach them with deference, you're likely to have a good result when invoking them for your work. Remember, remember, to write down everything. I say it all the time, but it is my favorite piece of advice for witches. If you don't write down what you did, you're not going to be able to replicate it, or to make specific changes for next time. You have to have a recipe before you can start making adjustments according to your taste.

When it comes to magick, the best thing you can be is bold and experimental. Be willing to fail, and that's how you're going to see the best results. Trial and error are the cornerstone of becoming a more confident witch. The more willing you are to stretch beyond what you find in spell books and what you read online, the more you're going to find yourself creating powerful, original magick.

Earth Magick: And last but certainly not least, we come to earth magick. Earth magick in particular feels very natural to me, and I use it all the time, probably more than other forms of elemental magick combined. Earth magick is very restorative, it's very comforting, very profound, and its results are very long-lasting and far-reaching.

Tailoring your spells to your exact desired outcome is tricky to do at first, but I have found that one of the best and most surefire ways to get really damn close is to remember to blend in the elements along with everything else. So while incorporating fire into your spell can give it an intense, blistering, quick-acting quality, incorporating earth magick can impart a deep, growing, building, long-lasting result.

So what kinds of spellwork are especially predisposed toward earth magick?

Spells having to do with health and wellness, first and probably foremost, as well as money, career, and abundance spells. This is because earth magick has a lot of influence over the things of the world, i.e. this mortal, earthly existence. Earth magick is also great for death and bone magick.

Another strong earth correspondence is protection magick, whether it's protection for yourself or a loved one, or protection for your home. Grounding and spending time in nature as restorative practices are also incredibly earth-centric.

For protection spells, amulets and talismans are particularly nice because they're easy to conceal, they can be made from just about anything from coins, to jewelry, to stones, and they're made to carry on your person.

Amulets and talismans are terms that are basically interchangeable, although if you're especially pedantic, you'll want to know that generally, an amulet is some sort of charm or token that confers protection on its user, whereas a talisman gives its user some kind of additional power, although the power given is usually protection, which is why the terms are swapped out so often.

But anyway, those kinds of charms are steeped in earth magic. Same with protection work that you do for your home. You can enchant windchimes, you can get some witch bells for your doorways, you can imbue nails or railroad spikes with protection magick and place them at the entryways or in the four corners of your property. Another form of protection I like, and one that I use in my own home, is hag stones in the windowsills.

Hag stones are rocks that have had holes bored through them by running water. You can sometimes find them in riverbeds, but I have always found them on the beach. If you do collect hag stones from nature, be sure that you leave something behind in return.

Hag stones are said to ward off evil when placed in window sills, and it's also said that if you look through the hole in them, you can see fairies and spirits. I have a small hag stone that I wear as a pendant whenever I feel like I need a little extra protection during my day. I also like amber, petrified wood, acorns, obsidian, and anything made of iron for home and personal space protection, like my car.

For health and wellness, when we are talking about earth magick, we are talking about plant medicine and herbs, elixirs, salves, tinctures, potions and balms. The reason I like to harp on herbal medicine IN ADDITION to herbal magick is because they are two completely different disciplines, yet they complement each other really beautifully.

There's a reason that herbs are part and parcel of witchcraft and it's because, historically, medicine men and women, shaman, witch doctors, curanderos, folk medicine practitioners, whatever you want to call these traditional healers, have folded magick and herbalism together to perform very effective treatments.

These people were well-respected within their communities for good reason. They had generations of knowledge of the plant medicines that grew in their regions and how to use them, and they were often the only people in their communities who could be called upon when medical emergencies came up.

All that said, I am not advocating for people to go off their meds, so don't write to me. I'm simply advocating for people to take an active role in their physical well-being. There are a lot of ways to support your physical health, but herbalism and getting outside in nature are two very powerful and simple ways to do that, and they are both, not surprisingly, earth magick. The earth gives so much to us, and we really don't have to do a whole lot to take advantage of that generosity.

Let's talk about money spells, abundance and career magick. Now, the reason those are earth magick is because they have to do with our physical existence, our worldly well-being. We came into this world with nothing and we will leave with nothing, but there's no reason not to want to have some financial security in the interim.

Putting together an abundance spell is a lot of fun, in my experience, and there are a million spells out in the ether that you can look up, so I'll just talk about some of my favorite elements to use in money magick.

As far as stones and minerals, I like pyrite a lot. It's probably my favorite stone to use. I also like peridot, tiger's eye, topaz, and red jasper. I've had great results with all of those and I think they work very quickly and easily.

As for herbs and plants, I like bay laurel, basil, olive, chamomile, dill, poppy, and even rice. Acorns are nice, and so are peonies and snapdragons for the altar. Precious metals like gold and silver are also great to adorn your altar space with for the duration of the work.

Magick is just like any other artform. You can learn to sing a song in foreign language, but if you translate it first, you'll be able to connect to the meaning in a personal way, and your performance will be all the more meaningful. And that's all that magick is. It's just singing our desires to the universe in a langage the universe understands.

SIGILS

All a sigil truly is, is any symbol that's used in magic. Traditionally, sigils were the occult symbols of angels or demons, and would be used by practitioners to exert some measure of control over those entities, and thereby allow them to compel the angel or the demon perform some sort of work for and on behalf of the practitioner. I'm sure plenty of occult schools still use these kinds of sigils in these ways and I wish them the best of luck with that. But as I don't generally summon angels OR demons if I can help it, this isn't a method I can expand on without resorting to just straight up bullshitting you. And that is not how I roll.

Now chaos magicians saw what the mystery schools were doing with sigils and said, "Oh that's nice, but I'mma make it better." And the pioneering chaos magician Aspen Spare developed a method of condensing words and phrases into these stylized monograms that are then charged with the practitioner's energy and intention, and sent out into the universe by the magician to call in the desired outcome. Which is typically how most witches are using sigils these days, even if they're designing them in a different way.

The Spare method is probably the easiest way for a witch to get their feet wet in designing sigils, because it's so straightforward, and these sigils do tend to work very well. A very common variation of the Spare method is this: you first spend some time creating a simple phrase that evokes exactly what your desired outcome is. For example you may have a job interview coming up, so your phrase might be 'I get this job' which is very simple, but this is just an example.

So you'll write your phrase down on a sheet of paper. Then, go through the letters and cross out the vowels and any repeating consonants. So in my example we will eliminate the vowels, and then because there are two T's in that phrase, we'll cross one out. The letters that remain now are G T H S J and B.

We will then use those remaining letters and arrange them in some sort of monogram-style design. We can overlap them or interconnect them, and generally just play around with the letters until we come up with a design that is visually pleasing for us, or that makes the impression we're looking for. Take your time with this step. We don't want to stop playing with our design until we love it.

This part of the process can take days, and if it's a sigil for a very important spell or manifestation, there's nothing wrong with that. We want to feel as though the symbol we create is perfect for our purpose. If you're going to bother doing a spell for something, you may as well spend some time and effort on it. And don't wait until it's something big to do your first sigil, start small and get comfortable with the process.

Another way to do this that incorporates numerology and magick squares, is called the Lo Shu grid method. You may want to look online for video explanations for using this method, as it is difficult to describe in print. But once you see how it's done, you'll be able to use it right away. It isn't a difficult method to learn, its just very visual.

This method is a great way to fold another layer of magick into your intention, as you can experiment with the numerical values of different phrases until you find one that matches your desired outcome with its numerological correspondence.

Now, just so we're clear, you can make your sigil look any way you want. There does not actually need to be any part of the written word incorporated into your design for it to be effective. It is the individual witch who gives the sigil its meaning and decides how it's going to be used and what it's going to represent. So if you meditate with your phrase or intention for a while and an image just comes to you, use that. Or you can try a form of automatic writing where you sit with some paper and a pen and just think about your desired outcome and let your pen flow over the page until an image emerges.

Another way to create a sigil that I am fond of (because visually and artistically, I am not super creative), is to borrow from existing symbolism. You can use planetary and zodiac symbols, alchemical symbols, runes, hieroglyphs, Celtic symbolism, you can draw on your own ethnic heritage and look for meaningful symbols there. You can incorporate numerology, simplified drawings of animals, tarot card imagery, you can create a literal drawing of the thing you're manifesting. If you're manifesting a new apartment, you might just draw a super basic house shape.

The point is, it doesn't matter what the symbol IS, it only matters that the symbol represents something specific TO YOU. So again, spend some time creating the design, draw it, erase it, change it, add to it, subtract from it. When you find the design that works, you'll know it.

And now that you've got the perfect sigil, it's time to charge it. This process is important because now that we have the symbol we want, we need to give it power and meaning. So draw your final symbol on a clean sheet of paper and choose your favorite charging method.

You can charge your symbol however you like, there is no right or wrong way. And you can meditate with it, you can charge it with crystals, you can charge it in sunlight, moonlight, even using your own orgasms is a really powerful way to charge your sigil.

And I wanted to mention, when you draw your final sigil, the one you want to finalize, so to speak, consider drawing it with charged ink.. You can dip a fingertip or a paint brush into the ink to draw your sigil.

Charged Witch's Ink

Combine ashes from old spells, burnt incense, ashes left over from ritual fire pits, or your own fireplace, in a jar. Add ground herbs and powdered incense specific to your intent, if desired. Add a few drops of essential oils that are meaningful to your intentions, if desired. Stir in a small amount of moonwater or Florida water into the ash mixture until you have the consistency you want.

So anyway, your sigil is created, you've drawn it, and you've charged it. Now what? Well, the cool thing is that now, you can do whatever you want to do with it. For a lot of witches, the sigil itself is the culmination of the spell.

For these witches, all of the psychic energy created, from the first moment of meditating about the intention, to the research into the symbols or shapes they use, to the design process, the trial and error of discovering the final sigil itself, to the charging of the sigil, that is for them the actual spell.

But depending on the purpose of the sigil, you may want to use it differently. You can carve your sigil into a candle, if you plan to use candle magick for your spell. You can write it in a small piece of paper and add it to a spell jar or mojo bag.

If the intent of the sigil is directed at a specific target, like a business where you would like to work, or the home of a person who's been pissing you off, you can write this sigil on a nearby sidewalk or a tree using chalk. If your sigil is a personal power symbol, you can use it in any of the ways we already described, or you can draw it on your body.

For many witches though, the last step is just to burn their sigil. This allows all of the energy they've created to pour out into the universe and begin to call in their manifestation. And let me assure you, this is very effective. If this is what you decide to do with your sigil, I don't think you'll be disappointed.

I have a power sigil that I like to use when I'm going to be in a situation when I feel like I might want a little extra confidence, and I like to draw it in dragon's blood oil on my wrists or over my solar plexus chakra (which is associated with self-confidence and self-esteem). If your sigil is for a health-related issue, you might draw it on your skin over the corresponding part of your body where your condition originates.

If your sigil is, for example, to increase or intensify your psychic abilities, you might draw it on your third eye with vitamin E oil, or even your regular moisturizer. Sigils for increasing beauty are drawn on the face in either moisturizer or concealer before being blended in. Witches will draw sigils on the soles of their shoes as a symbolic way of helping them literally get to their manifestations. Sigils are kept in wallets to increase wealth.

I have a sigil on my laptop to help me in my work. Trace your sigil into your coffee with your spoon. Put a sigil under your pillow for better sleep, or maybe prophetic dreams, put one under your mattress to make your relationship stronger. I'm going to get a couple emails explaining to me that sigils are meant to be burnt and that's it, and using them any other way just treats them like a talisman. And while I agree, sort of, I also don't care about arguing the semantics.

A talisman is basically a good luck charm engraved with some sort of protective symbol. Talismans are very useful, very effective, and I personally have several that I use for different applications. But the sigil is so much more personalized and therefore customizable for just about any purpose, and it aids the witch who made it in manifesting something very specific to that witch. It isn't a general use, multipurpose symbol. It is so much more.

And that's why I don't mind using the term sigil to describe them, even when they're used differently to how they were originally devised.

ABUNDANCE MAGICK

I wanted to talk about abundance magick and manifestations, especially on the heels of talking about earth magick. These two terms, abundance and manifestation, have really grown in usage as the New Age movement and Witchcraft have merged in recent years.

Or, maybe merge isn't the word I want, because there is still a lot of difference between the two, but they have definitely overlapped. It's more of a Venn diagram than a merger. What we call manifestation now used to just be spellwork. You wouldn't say, "I'm manifesting a better job" you would just say, "I cast a spell to find a better job."

I don't really know exactly when the crossover took place, but it did, and now the term manifestation is ubiquitous in witchcraft. And that's fine, I don't really care, I just want to make it clear for the purposes of this book that I will be using manifestation and spellwork interchangeably.

The term abundance is another one that comes to us from the New Age movement and popular psychology as well. It is a well-known psychological phenomenon that people who approach life with an abundance mindset will almost always have better outcomes and better overall mental and even physical health versus folks with a scarcity mindset. It's quantifiable.

And we can take it a step further when we associate it with the placebo effect. The placebo effect refers to the beneficial effects of a treatment that has nothing to do with the treatment itself and only comes about because of the patient's belief in that treatment. And it never fails to blow my mind that doctors will literally dismiss a positive result based on the placebo effect without acknowledging that the patient's mindset literally improved their own health.

It's so remarkable to me that western medicine in particular hates to acknowledge that. And I understand why; you can't charge a copay for a placebo. But what we call placebo is really just the mind creating its own reality. And that's all that magick is when it comes right down to it.

We can apply that concept to literally every aspect of witchcraft if we want to. We always say that the magick isn't in the crystals or the herbs or the cauldron, or the moon phase; these things are inert without the power of the witch. And there is so much truth to that. I believe that the crystals, herbs, and rituals help to support the magick, but the witch makes the magick happen.

So let's talk about supporting ourselves in our manifestations, our spellwork, by creating and cultivating an abundance mindset. First, we are going to identify the things that we already have that are going to help to call in what it is we are trying to manifest.

So for example, if we want to manifest a better job, we can focus on all the qualities we have that are going to make us perfect for that new position. Instead of approaching it from a position of scarcity, where we are fixated on our fear of being unqualified for it, or maybe we are concerned we don't have enough experience for it, or whatever, we can instead start focusing on, or visualizing, how great we are going to be at this new job once we get it.

We have to be our own hype man and talk to ourselves about all the ways we are going to be brilliant at it. When we align our thoughts that way, we are creating our own placebo effect, if you will. The mind begins to believe and to create the reality wherein we are perfect for this job, so *of course* we are going to get it. Or whatever the goal is.

This practice can also help us by making us see possibilities that we wouldn't normally see. We all know about the The Baader-Meinhof Phenomenon, otherwise known as the frequency illusion or recency bias. In an oversimplified nutshell, this is when you see or learn something new, and then you suddenly start seeing it everywhere. The mind is really good at seeing what it wants to see.

It's also really good at ignoring what it doesn't want to see. And this effect correlates with why people who we think of as negative, or pessimistic, or glass half empty types, will bitch relentlessly about all the bad things going on in their lives and completely ignore all the good things in their lives. They are only seeing what they want to see.

Every inconvenience, no matter how big or small, just reinforces their belief that the world is out to get them and nothing ever goes their way. And it really doesn't even matter if good things do happen, because they either don't pay attention to it, or they only focus on the potentially negative aspects of it. Like if they do get a job opportunity, they won't even take it because they are convinced it will probably just end up sucking anyway, or it's too inconvenient to change jobs, or maybe the morning commute will be a bit longer.

These people will turn that potential opportunity into yet another example of how nothing ever goes right for them. They'll sincerely say things like, "See? Even when I finally get a job offer, it was even worse than my current job!" They all but create these conditions.

And because their minds are ignoring anything positive, their reality is such that they are constantly living in a state of scarcity. Even if there are in fact things that they can be grateful for, they are unable to recognize it; they only see the bad things. And those people are often really miserable to be around for the rest of us, because they don't only see the negatives in their own lives, but in others as well. These people can be very critical towards others. And on the rare occasion when they do recognize that something good has happened to someone else, they are incapable of being happy for them. Because of the very nature of a scarcity mindset, it makes them feel that if something goes well for someone else, that now there's even less for the rest of us.

Now. This is where I backtrack a whole bunch and explain that I am not saying that everything bad that happens to us is all our fault, or that we've invited the misfortunes that befall us. Because unfortunately, bad things happen to good people all the time, and it isn't their fault. I am not victim blaming. Accidents and illness and shitty people can make victims of us all. What I am talking about has more to do with how we choose to interpret our circumstances.

But the good news is that we can use the Baader-Meinhof phenomenon, which is something the brain always does anyway, to our advantage. What I mean by this is that when we program our minds, for lack of a better word, to look for ways to get the things we want, to look for opportunities, we are going to notice them more and more, and we are going to start seeing opportunities that we might miss if we weren't being open and receptive to those opportunities.

So that all just kind of covers the theory of abundance magick and manifestation and why it works. I mean, that's my theory at least, I don't mean to imply that it's some kind of universal truth. But understanding the 'why' of it isn't a guaranteed fast track to understanding the 'how' of it. Like anything else, it takes practice and patience.

Now, there is also the fact that once we cast a spell, we also have to just trust that our intentions are out there and the Universe is listening and working on getting us what we've called in. And I'm not trying to undermine that, because as the saying goes, once you plant a seed, it doesn't help if you dig it up everyday to check if it's growing yet. That's not what I'm suggesting here.

What I'm saying is that when we do our spellwork, we need to be ready to see its results when they begin to appear to us. While it doesn't help to dwell or ruminate on getting the results you want from your spellwork after you've cast it, it does help to be open to receiving the results in whichever manner they may come.

Finally, be generous with yourself in your manifestations. I think that we sometimes are afraid to ask for too much. Whether we are worried we don't deserve it, or we're afraid if we dream too big we won't get it, and we will end up disappointed, or if it's some other reason entirely, just stop that.

Quit minimizing the blessings that you're willing to receive. The Universe is so vast. The earth is so generous. There is plenty out there for all of us. Get out of the scarcity mindset, and start allowing yourself to receive abundance, in whatever way you define it. I just want everyone who reads these words to know that you deserve to have everything you've ever wanted. You are a divine soul, you are a brilliant point of light in the Universe, and I am privileged to be alive in this body at the same time as you, so that I can remind you that you are a magician. And I can't wait to see the magick you create.

That's enough theory and rote definition. Let's look at some spells we can work to call in abundance. Specifically, money. This is not the only definition of abundance, and it isn't even the most important, but the fact is that we are living in a material world, and we are all material girls. Or boys, or others.

Money Magick Candle Spell

Carve a green candle with symbols that align with your intention, such as dollar signs or runes, or simply carve a dollar amount right into the wax.. Anoint the candle with money drawing oil (recipe below). Sprinkle the oiled candle with ground ginger or ground cinnamon, taking care to rub the spice into the carvings. Fix your candle securely into a candle holder.

Place your hands on either side of the candle and focus your energy on your desire. Blast as much energy as you can through the palms of your hand into the candle. Once you feel as through the candle has been sufficiently charged, light it and let it burn down safely

←〈〉→

Money Drawing Oil

While focusing on your intention, combine cinnamon, crushed bay leaves, basil, echinacea, lemongrass oil, lavender, orange peel, cayenne pepper, star anise, cedar, chamomile, clove, comfrey, dill, mandrake root, mint, nutmeg, pine, sesame and an ounce of Florida water. Add everything to a small saucepan and cover with about 2oz of hemp or olive oil.

Warm over very low heat for 30 minutes or so, stirring often. Remove from heat, cool, and add to a small jar or bottle with some peridot chips and a small pinch of blessed money clippings (instructions below). Leave out anything you don't have, and make substitutions as necessary. Once everything is combined, charge your oil for use in your spells.

Blessed Money Clippings

Get a dollar bill, preferably one with repeating digits in the serial number, especially 7s. . Cleanse the bill with smoke from either sage or incense, and then bless and sanctify it for the purpose of calling in more money to yourself. Cut the cleansed and blessed bill into confetti-sized pieces and keep them in a small ziploc baggie or container. Add a small pinch of the clippings to any spellwork having to do with money, including mojo bags, spell jars, candle rituals, and oils. You'll be able to do several spells with one dollar bill.

Bay Laurel Manifestation

Probably the simplest form of manifestation, simply write your desire on a bay leaf, charge it, and then and then burn it. You can incorporate the elements into your spell by releasing the ashes into the wind, in flowing water, or you by burying them.

Road Opener Candle Spell

This spell is meant to remove roadblocks or obstacles toward your desired manifestation. To begin, get a candle, white is fine, but you may prefer to use orange for opportunity or green for success if you have access to colored candles. Carve your intentions into the wax. You can use runes, or a sigil of your own design, or you can just carve words into it.

Dress the candle with olive oil. In a mortar, crush allspice, star anise or some dried orange peel for luck, and cinnamon, ginger or lemon balm for success, and mistletoe or wormwood to remove obstacles. Rub the herb mixture onto the surface of the candle while envisioning your outcome. Charge your candle with your energy and light it. Allow your candle to burn down, and of course, never leave your burning candle unattended.

Manifestation Oil

This is a general purpose oil to use for any manifestation workings, and it's customizable. Into your saucepan, pour 2 oz. of your carrier oil, such as olive oil. Add one bay leaf, a teaspoon of rosemary, chamomile, patchouli, and dragon's blood resin. Warm through on low heat for 20-30 minutes, then strain the herbs out and pour the oil into a small bottle or jar.

PROTECTION MAGICK

P rotection magick is just a really important skill to practice and try to master, almost before any other kind of magic. We need to be able to create a bubble around ourselves, our loved ones, our home, our vehicle, our workspace, and our altar. Especially as witches.

We dabble, manipulate, and interact with all kinds of energies, and this draws a lot of attention from beyond the veil. We are a beacon of energetic light to all kinds of beings, both worldly and otherworldly, and we need to be prepared for the kinds of spiritual moths that our light attracts.

We have to keep any nasty, funky, ugly energy off of us as much as we can. Now we can't protect ourselves from everything, but it's so important to practice good spiritual hygiene. Brushing your teeth twice a day may not prevent every single tiny little cavity, but Jesus, imagine the state of your teeth if you never brushed them.

So with that in mind, we are going to tackle different kinds of protection magick and how, exactly, to use them. First and foremost, before we ward ourselves or our spaces, we need to cleanse. Wards won't kick things out; they'll just prevent new things from getting in. So we'll need to do a cleansing first, and then throw our wards to keep any new buggers from getting in.

Cleansing can be done in a variety of ways for a variety of needs. Smoke cleansing is probably the way we're most familiar with, and this just entails opening our windows and doors, lighting herbs or incense and wafting the smoke throughout our space, usually beginning from the back of the home and moving toward the front, while stating our intent firmly and clearly. We'll want to waft our smoke up into the corners and in the closets.

We don't want to leave anywhere for the nasties to hide. If smoke isn't allowed or isn't advised for any reason, you can also make a cleansing spray.

Protection Spray

First, make some moon water. For this moon water, we will set the intention of protection. In addition to water, place some cleansing and purifying herbs in the jar as well. Herbs such as rosemary, basil, cedar, juniper, sage, thyme, and lavender work well. If you have other herbs that you'd like to add, especially if you feel prompted by Spirit or your own intuition, by all means add those too.

You can add some cleansing stones to your water as well, as long as they're water safe. Some of my favorites for this work are clear quartz, amethyst, agate, tiger's eye and black obsidian. Again, if there are other stones you feel called to use, don't let me stop you. But please do a Google search ahead of time and make sure that they're safe to use in water. Crystals aren't cheap; I'd hate for anyone to ruin their beloved crystals with water. I also recommend adding some salt to this water. Not a lot, just a pinch. It's so cleansing, and it can really kick up the power a notch.

That's all there is to it; place your water outside or on a windowsill overnight in full view of the moon and it'll be ready to use in the morning. Now, some witches will suggest doing this on the full moon so that you get the full power of the moon in your water. Others will suggest waiting for the new moon since you're using the water for banishing. I say either method is fine, just pick your favorite. In the morning, strain out your herbs and put the water into a spray bottle. You can leave the stones in there if you like, since they won't get sucked up into the little spray mechanism. Then you'll just proceed throughout your home as you would if you were using smoke; open the windows and just spritz the shit out of all the negative or oppressive freeloaders in your space.

←◇→

If you can't do this to your entire home for whatever reason, maybe you have roommates that don't approve or maybe you're still living with your parents, you can certainly do it to your own bedroom at least. What's really great about the water method is that it's so versatile, and it's discreet.

If you're not so worried about roommates or parents, but you're still not down with smoke or water, you can also just use your own energy to get rid of unwanted entities. The way we do this is to raise a bunch of energy in our space and literally shout those bastards out of our house. Because as we constantly hear, the tools aren't where the magick comes from; the magick comes from the witch.

So turn on some music that raises your personal vibrations, turn it on good and loud. Start dancing. And I mean, really move your body. This isn't going on YouTube, so don't worry about how you look. Don't even think about how you look. Just start calling in energy, get those muscles warm, when you're really in the zone and you feel like you're at the peak of that energy bubble, grab a bell or a drum or even just a pot and a wooden spoon and just start banging the hell out of it. Make a ton of racket and start commanding those unwanted entities to LEAVE your space.

Once you've cleansed the space, place sigils on your doors and windows (more about this in the Sigils chapter). This can be any sigil you've made, it can be a preexisting, well-known symbol, like a pentacle or even a cross, if that resonates with you. To place the sigils, you can use the same moon water you already made, if that's the method you used, or you can use Florida water, or holy water if you happen to have some. Anyway, dab some of the liquid of your choice on your fingertip and draw your sigils while repeating your protective mantra, whatever it may be. You can also use chalk, or you can just light incense and trace your sigil in the air a few inches from the windows or doors.

Florida Water

Into a large mason jar, place a sprig of rosemary, and one tablespoon each of the following: juniper berries, whole cloves, cedar, sweetgrass, lavender, rose petals, orange peel, mint, and basil. Pour 2 pints of cheap vodka into the jar and close it tightly with a lid. Give it a good shake and place it in a dark cabinet. Shake it once daily for a full moon cycle (28 days), then strain out the herbs and discard them. Put your florida water back into the jar or a bottle and use as needed.

←◇→

So. Now your space is cleansed, your doors and windows have been sigilized, and next we have to lock the building or room or space down tight and make sure none of those little beasties come back. For this, we are going to make and set wards. You can turn anything into a ward.

Some of the wards around our home, just to give you an idea, are some metal windchimes in the backyard, a set of witch bells at the front door, hag stones on several windowsills, crystals on several other windowsills, a spell jar that's buried near the front walkway, a large metal coin that I keep in my car, a jar of black salt in my office at work, and some iron railroad spikes buried at the four corners of our property. And that's not even all of them.

A ward can be made of almost anything. Its purpose is just to house the protective energy that you put into it and to release that energy over a period of time to protect your space.

So to make some object into a ward, first, choose your object. It can be a cool stone you find, it can be a handful of acorns from your morning walk through the park, it can be something you've bought, like a windchime.

I find that some objects are better at housing energy than others; natural materials seem to hold energy longer and work a bit better, but your experience may vary. Especially if the object you've chosen has special sentimental value. This is where you as the witch need to make the judgment call for yourself.

Protective Wards

Cleanse the item you've chosen as your ward in the same way you cleansed your space. Smoke, water, whatever you choose. Then, jam as much protective energy that you can create into the object. For this, you're going to draw the energy into yourself first. So at your altar or other private space, light a candle and set your object in front of it.

Close your eyes if it helps, and envision this energy being pulled into your body through the palms of your hands, moving through your arms, into your torso. A blinding, white-hot ball of energy inside your chest, building and getting bigger and stronger and hotter. Then just blast that energy back out through your palms into the object.

←◇→

You're going to make as many wards as you think you'll need, and then place them where you want them, such as near the points of entry to your home or space, or on your front and back porch. In or near your office or vehicle, your locker, in your purse or wallet too, so that you carry that protection with you.

Check in with your wards periodically, because they will need to be charged from time to time. And if you have a ward that gets to the point that you feel like it's just done all that it can for you, thank it for its protection, and retire it. If it's something natural, you can return it to nature. If it's something that doesn't work as a ward anymore but still holds sentimental value, then just keep it.

That should be sufficient to keep out most mundane forms of unwanted energy or entities. You can repeat this process as needed to keep yourself and your spaces cleared, and rest easily.

As a witch, even if you never do anything bad in your whole life and are a total lightworker and you never do baneful magick and you're the world's best healer, the very FACT of your magick is going to attract all kinds of attention from the spirit world. And not all of that attention is going to be welcome. The same light that attracts guardian angels will attract negative entities too. So it's best to be prepared, and I hope you feel prepared.

Even if your home currently feels totally clear, just do a cleansing to practice it. It can't hurt to have the experience under your belt so that in the event, goddess forbid, you ever DO feel attacked or compromised, you will have the confidence to clean your own house and set those magical boundaries so that it is less likely to happen again.

LOVE MAGICK

N ow I have said before that I don't do love magick to fix relationships in which one person is a cheating bastard, or doesn't treat their partner right in general. I am not interested in doing magick to try and get decent treatment out of someone shitty. That's not the kind of magick we are going to talk about here.

We are going to talk about magick for putting a little spice back into an established relationship, we will talk about magick for finding love if you happen to be a single witch, and we will also talk about magick for self-love, which is really the most potent form of love magick we can do.

When we are radiating self-love, when true, deep, all-encompassing self-love is emanating from us, we really become irresistible. People are drawn to us, it's magnetic. Think about the most charismatic person you have ever known. Think about why that person was able to draw others in. Whoever this person is that you're thinking of was probably not constantly putting themselves down. This is probably a confident person. Not cocky, but self-assured.

This is such an important aspect of attracting others, and not just in a romantic way, but in general. So even though I think we sometimes hear self-love magick and think eh, that's lame, that just could not be further from the truth. So we are going to talk about that too.

Now the thing about self-love magick in particular, is that it's going to be very individualized. Only you know where your self-love blockages lie, you know what I mean?

If you're having difficulty feeling very loving and powerful and enamored of yourself, you're going to have to do a little introspection and sort of home in what you think that you're not bringing to the table, and stop making whatever those issues are, larger than they need to be. Once you are able to be honest and look at yourself objectively you'll be able to identify those areas where you need to lift yourself up.

And the easiest way to do that is to think of yourself the way you would think of a friend. If you had a friend who was very down on him or herself, who felt like the reason they couldn't find someone special was because they didn't deserve it, it would probably be easy for you to identify those areas of insecurities and tell your friend why they're amazing anyway.

And we have to do that shit for ourselves too. So, before you begin self-love work, or rather, as the first step in performing this kind of work, get a sheet of paper and a pen and ask yourself honestly what you think you may need to focus on, and then based on that list, we can start to develop a spell.

HOWEVER, this doesn't mean that we are working a spell to change a bunch of stuff about ourselves. If one of the things on my list is that I feel like I won't find love until I lose this last 15 pounds, I'm not going to do a weight loss spell and call it a self-love spell. Because that isn't the same thing.

I can love myself and respect myself and recognize that I am worthy of a healthy, loving relationship AND ALSO have some goals for myself that I haven't met yet. We are all a work in progress. None of us is perfect and we can't hold ourselves to that kind of standard.

So when I say to write down what you want to focus on, I might add to that list self-acceptance, self-forgiveness, and self-confidence. Spells for self-love are not spells to change a bunch of things.

This is a spell to love myself, along with all of my flaws. And it is a spell to recognize all of the good things about me that I am proud of and that I think I do well. So we are going to add those things to our list as well. And finally, we are going to add to our list those things that we intend to manifest for ourselves.

And I'm not talking about you know, that promotion at work, or a new apartment or something, I mean things you want to manifest for your spiritual or emotional wellbeing. The purpose of this list is to write a spell, essentially a love letter, to yourself. You're going to pour your heart out to the universe, you're going to describe yourself in glowing terms. You are writing about yourself the way that you would write about someone you love and admire.

You can address this spell to the universe, to Spirit, to a particular deity that you work with, or even to the moon, which is how I've addressed the example spell I've created. If you're especially poetic, you can make it rhyme, but if you're not especially poetic, as I am not, you don't have to worry about it. So once we've got everything written down, we can play with the wording until we are happy with it, and end up with something like this:

My beloved moon,

I am Eli, and I stand in awe of your beauty and in gratitude for your love.

I am kind, and I am loving. I am a good friend, I am thoughtful, I am creative, I am compassionate, I attract good people into my life. I am generous, and I am resilient.

I learn and grow every day. I help others, and I accept help from others when I am in need of it. I become more powerful and more wise with every passing year. I have a wonderful family, and I am surrounded by people who love me. I love myself, and I love who I will yet become.

This is my vow. So mote it be.

Now the important thing, when you're working your self-love spell, is to make sure that everything you say, all of the things from your list, including everything that you want to become, and everything you like about yourself that you already are, is spoken in the same present tense, as if it's already all true. As if you've already become the person you're trying to create. This is important and it's the same thing we do in every kind of spell; speak it as if it's already yours.

So when you read the little example spell I wrote, you can't tell the difference between what is already true about me and what I am still working on, what I'm trying to manifest. And the Universe doesn't know the difference either; you speak those wonderful qualities about yourself and the Universe believes you, so it helps to make it so.

So we have our written spell (of course, you're going to use your own words), what else do we need? Well that depends on what we want to draw in. If you want to use herbs, crystals or oils to match your specific self-love intentions, then you need to identify what those intentions are.

If we wrote confidence on our list, we might want to use cedar, oak, rosemary, agate, obsidian, or tiger's eye, if we want to manifest more self-acceptance, we will use mustard, ruby, or clover, and if we want self-forgiveness, we might try geranium, wormwood, rhodonite, or apache tears.

Now if you're a single witch looking to find a companion of some kind, there are a lot of elements for attraction spells, such as dragon's blood, both the oil and the incense work very well, also chamomile, jasmine, strawberry, mandrake, and vanilla, amber, moonstone, and topaz. Any of those elements, or a combination, will work beautifully for candle spells, particularly red or green candles. They will also work nicely in a ritual bath.

You can word your spell however you like, of course, but be specific about the qualities that you're looking for in a partner, and be specific about what kind of partnership you're trying to manifest as well.

If you're just interested in a dating situation, nothing necessarily long-term, just something kind of casual, then say so in your spell. If you are looking for something more serious, then you will want to say that too. There are 8 billion people on this planet; whatever it is you're looking for, that person is out there. But you'll have to call for them, so the more specifically you word your petition, the more likely you are to get someone who is a good fit for you.

When you are figuring out the wording in your spell, consider that you may want to describe this person first of all, as if they are already here, but also think about it like this: imagine that you've already met this person, and you're describing them to your best friend. So you're going to say things like, he is so thoughtful, he's really considerate, he's kind, we have a lot in common, he is such a great listener, etc.

You're talking about this person in the present tense as if you already have this person in your life.

And again, once you've got your shopping list of qualities in a partner, you're going to want to use materials in your spell that correspond with those qualities. So your partner is kind, maybe some allspice and jade, your partner is optimistic, perhaps juniper and citrine, they are successful, how about lemon balm and carnelian. Maybe your partner is passionate, so you'll use coriander and opal. And if your partner is generous, try honeysuckle and cat's eye.

And by the way, yes, there are definitely ethical considerations that go into any kind of love spell work. But I'm not here to lecture you; I am disseminating this information with the understanding that you are responsible for your own spellwork and any backlash that may come of it.

If you're going to do a love spell to get the attention of someone you already know, someone you want to date and that person is already in a relationship, well, that's messy and gross and I don't recommend it. But it's also your problem, so proceed with caution and don't say I didn't warn you.

Now if you are already in a relationship and all you're really interested in doing is putting some fire back into the physical aspect of that relationship, we are going to put together a love oil.

Igniting Passion Oil

In a small saucepan, pour 2oz skin-safe oil such as vitamin E oil or almond oil. To this, add a few drops each of cinnamon essential oil for lust, passionflower oil for attraction, and rose oil for love. Add ¼ tsp vanilla for its aphrodisiac qualities, a little frankincense to add a spiritual quality to the experience, and about ½ tsp of rose petals for love, apple blossoms for happiness, or violets for lust. Steep your oil for 20-30 minutes and let cool. Strain out your plant materials and our your oil into a small bottle or jar. Add a small amethyst and rose quartz to the finished oil.

←◇→

Disclaimer here right off the top: if you're going to use this oil to anoint your candles or put in spell jars or something, you can just use the essential oils themselves. However, if you plan to use this oil for massage, or to draw sigils or symbols onto your own body or onto your lover's body, you must dilute the essential oils in a skin-safe carrier oil, like almond oil or vitamin E, and just use a couple drops of each essential oil and DO NOT use these oils directly on your genitals.

So to get this whole experience going, to put it all together, I'd anoint a red candle with our passion oil, I might carve some symbols or sigils into it, I might even just carve hearts into the wax to keep it simple. Crush some of the herbs we used in our oil and roll the anointed candle into them, and light the candle with intention. We want this to be an especially spicy, passionate night to remember.

And let me assure you, if you tell your partner that you've created this oil and what it's meant to do, it's basically a self-fulfilling prophecy. You're going to get some spice. But you don't have to tell them. It will work anyway.

BANEFUL MAGICK

One thing a lot of newer witches are iffy about is cursing people. Hexes, jinxes, curses, banishing, etc. What we typically think of as being associated with evil. A lot of witches are concerned about the rule of three, others think that if someone crosses you, they deserve what they get. Now, here is my take on that: do what you want, I don't give a shit.

I am not a Wiccan or a lightworker, and I have cast and still will cast not-so-nice spells in situations where I feel like it's warranted. My only concern for newer witches is this: consider the worst case scenario before you begin to perform that spell. By that I mean, if this spell were to go horribly wrong and blow up in your face, what would that look like?

As with all spellwork, but especially with baneful work, be very, VERY specific with your intention and consider the possibilities if your spell goes tits up. Cast protective wards beforehand so that your spell is less likely to rebound on you, and then go on with your bad self.

I don't hex lightly and I don't hex often, but I do hex. And I think it's important to note that just because we are willing to hex someone doesn't mean we are necessarily willing to hex everyone. And by and large, as long as we keep powerful wards on ourselves, we kind of don't need to hex too often.

I'm sure it's happened to a lot of us: when someone is going out of their way to make our lives miserable, be it a hateful coworker or spiteful in-law, oftentimes things seem to work out that the person who is working so hard against us ends up reaping what they've sown, without us having to do much at all.

I'm going to be deliberately vague here, but I personally have dealt with a couple individuals who seemed determined to make my life a living hell and although they did give me grief for a while, eventually their own lives completely fell apart without my intervention whatsoever.

I had a boss several years ago who was just awful to work for. And I'm talking sexual harassment, unreasonable demands, he was racist, he was a narcissist, he was dishonest, etc, etc. And I struggled for a long time with working for him, because I was very new in that field, and I didn't have the resources or the connections to strike out on my own, and he had been doing that work for a long time and could very easily ruin my reputation and make it impossible to work in that field, at least in my town.

And to be very honest, I was making a lot of money working for him. So I just didn't know what to do or where to go for help, especially because, although I was working for him and under him, I was technically an independent contractor.

But it got to the point where I was losing sleep, I was having panic attacks, it was affecting my mental and physical health, and I just had to walk away. I was forced to acknowledge that, even if it meant I couldn't work in that field anymore, which hurt a lot because it was not easy to get licensed to do that work, that it wasn't worth the compromises I was having to make with my health, my dignity and my ethics.

So I wrote a resignation letter in which I detailed all the awful things he had done that contributed to my decision to leave, and I walked away and never looked back. I stayed friends with another woman who was working for him at the time, and a or so month later I learned that she had quit on him too, that he had lost an enormous part of his business due to his own sloppy handling of it, and that his marriage was in trouble.

So that's what I mean when I say that most of the time, witches don't need to do anything. Shitty people tend to destroy themselves given time. But there are times when it would behoove a witch to intervene. And that's what this chapter is about.

Just as with other kinds of magic, there are a lot of methods. Spell jars, vinegar jars, sigils, bindings, and on and on. So I'm not going to necessarily give step-by-step instructions about how to do curses here, because there are plenty of hexes and curses to be found in books and online, but I will give a little practical advice and some general tips.

First and foremost, and this is true if you are going to do any magic, but especially baneful magic, make damn sure your wards and protective charms are in place, good and solid, and thoroughly charged.

You don't know what kind of reverberations may come back on you, even if the object of your hex isn't a witch, and even if you don't believe in karma or the three fold rule, which I don't. Sometimes, people just have the knack for sending back ill intentions even when they don't use magick, and even if they don't believe in magick. So keep your amulets and talismans healthy, and even do a special charm to protect yourself for the specific hex you're setting.

Next, be very specific about the hex or curse. And again, this is true of all spellwork. But if for example, you're cursing someone to lose their hair, make sure that your curse is worded in such a way that they aren't going to lose their hair from cancer, ok?

But by and large, magick works by taking the path of least

resistance. So if you're cursing someone so that they have relationship trouble, the simplest way for magick to do this might be for the person's partner to become gravely ill, or even to straight up die. So when you're writing your spell, word it very specifically. "Connor will break up with Jasmine forever" is specific. "Connor will leave Jasmine forever" is vague. Don't leave room for the Universe to interpret your words. Be clear in your intention.

Along that same line, set a timeline if it's appropriate for the spell. If you want your bitchy coworker to leave your company, you can work the best, most powerful spell ever, but if you don't set a timeline, you might be waiting for a while.

It goes along with the path of least resistance again. Maybe your coworker will leave... in five years when she hits retirement age. So maybe when you're writing your spell, set your intention to happen, say, by the next full moon, or by Lughnasadh, or whatever. Be clear, be specific, and consider any potential mix-ups with your wording or with the outcome.

So with that all said, let's talk just a little about what kinds of ingredients to put in your baneful spells! The typical things that come readily to mind are vinegar and lemon juice, but sometimes people use pickle juice, thorns, rusty nails, pins, razor blades, barbed wire, basically any sharp bits of old rusty metal, cat shit is a popular one, literal poison, like rat poison or insect poison.

I shouldn't have to warn you to be VERY careful with these. Don't touch this stuff with your bare hands, and if you do use these things in your spell work, make sure that your container is glass and has a secure lid.

Now, be very careful about mixing noxious chemicals because you don't want to accidentally gas yourself. Please take the utmost care about what you do with these items and where and how you dispose of them. We are trying to hex humans, not animals or the environment.

As far as herbs and plants to be used in curses and other baneful work, it should be kept in mind that a lot of the plants that we may use in beneficial work can also be used in baneful work as well. Their effect just depends on our intent, and how we charge the ingredients to let them know what we need from them.

The following is a (not at all comprehensive) list of some of the more commonly used herbs that are good for spell jars, spell bags, dressing candles, and whatever hexing method you prefer to use :

Cayenne pepper is great for causing anxiety and unease. It is a really good choice for making someone want to quit their job.

Castor beans can cause sickness or illness. Castor beans are also incredibly poisonous, so keep them out of reach of children and do not ingest them or give them to someone who might ingest them.

Chili powder can be used to cause discord in relationships and struggles in general.

Datura, which may only be easy to come by if you live somewhere where it grows wild, is excellent for causing nightmares, confusion and misery.

Hemlock is another great plant for sowing discord too.

Ivy is a great plant for doing bindings. Because of the way it grows, just wrapping around trees and pillars, and just choking out other plant life, it is a natural for that kind of work and works very well in that capacity.

Mistletoe will just straight up cause harm. Be very VERY specific how you set your intention with that one. And in fact, mistletoe, castor and datura are what I think of as pulling out the big guns.

Nightshade is a great plant for causing nightmares and restless sleep, so if you're just looking to make someone's life miserable in general, nightshade is the right herb for the job.

Stinging nettle will encourage jealousy and unhappiness in relationships.

And there you have it! Again, if you do use this kind of magick, please do so with the full understanding of what you're about to undertake. I am not responsible for any work that you do which comes back to bite you in the ass. We're all grown up witches here, so we have to behave that way.

Magick is amazing and it can be a lot of fun, but it can also be incredibly harmful if we're sloppy and careless. So don't be a messy witch! Hex responsibly.

Binding Spell

This spell is meant to bind another from harming others, both physically and emotionally. Into a glass jar with a tight-fitting lid, add a cutting of ivy, and one teaspoon each of fennel or garlic to guard against aggression, nettle to establish boundaries and set limitations, ground mustard (or whole mustard seed) or comfrey to eliminate enmity or hostility, and thyme and cumin to repel negativity.

Add a personal concern of the person being bound, such as hair, fingernail clippings, or a picture. Seal the jar shut, and wrap the jar with twine, string, or yarn. Wrap the jar several times, and with each wrap, repeat your command, something like, "[NAME], I bind you from harming me with your words and actions. Everytime you speak against me, you choke on your words." Once you're satisfied, bury the jar far from your property.

←◇→

Banishing Oil

Into a small saucepan, pour 2oz carrier oil, such as olive oil. Add to this a teaspoon of Witch Hazel, basil, pine needles, pepper, either ground or whole peppercorns, salt, and finally, star anise. Star anise acts as a natural pentacle and therefore endows your work with the protective qualities of a pentacle, and one of those properties is of course to drive away negativity.

Another note on banishing oil is that everything in this oil will also function beautifully as a protective oil. So if you don't need to banish anyone or anything, consider making some of this anyway and consecrating it for protection instead.

←◇→

ALTARS

ltars are such a wonderful tool, they're excellent for creating a sacred space to meditate or focus on a goal, or a manifestation, or to commune with a spirit guide, a deity, or a departed loved one. This can also be the place where we do our spell work, and where we keep a lot of our tools.

And, as with everything else we talk about here, there is no right or wrong way to create and use an altar. There are a lot of different kinds of altars and all of them are valid.

Some traditions do have prescribed altar arrangements and those are easy to look up online. Wicca has pretty specific parameters for an altar arrangement, but I'm not a Wiccan, so while my personal altars do typically have some things in common with a Wiccan altar, there are some significant differences as well. And of course, you can have several altars in your home at a given time.

I know witch named Candace who has her working altar, and then another out in the common area of her home, along with a seasonal altar, and then she keeps an altar for her little witches to tend, with imagery of whatever deity they happen to be learning about and working with, which is really cool.

I have a few altars myself. I have a working altar, I have a small altar on the mantle where I observe the seasons and sabbats, and

I've got a very small shelf where I display my daily tarot card and my weekly oracle card. It's definitely not a traditional altar, but it is an altar. It's a point of focus for my practice, it's a place I look to when I get a little overwhelmed and need to remember what the day has in store for me and, especially with my weekly oracle card, it reminds me not to go off the rails when something goes tits up during the week.

And all those altars look different and have different elements and are used differently. So again, no right or wrong way. But let's talk about some of the elements that we frequently find on a witch's altar.

Working altars are probably what most of us envision when we speak of altars, and this is going to be where we do a lot of our work, so we'll start there with the question of where to place the altar. In many traditions, the altar is oriented to face North, or is placed in the northern part of the room or the home. Sometimes this isn't possible or practical, so if North isn't gonna work for you, don't sweat it.

I've had a southern facing working altar for seven years and I have not noticed a difference in my magic. I could easily move it to the other side of my room, but the way it's positioned now it sits under a window and during significant moon cycles, it's exposed to direct moonlight that it would not receive otherwise. So the placement isn't traditional, but it isn't haphazard either. So again, consider all kinds of factors and make the correct decision for your space and your altar.

You may consider the correspondences of the different cardinal directions, North for example is associated with the element of earth, abundance, wealth and success, and manifestation. South is associated with the element of fire, ambition, creativity, love and sexuality, purification, rebirth and renewal.

East is associated with air, with communication, divination, wisdom, illumination, and powers of the mind. And finally west is associated with water, with the afterlife, dream work, emotions, psychic ability, and compassion. So, be mindful when you're placing your altar, certainly, but don't despair if you can't orient your altar to the North.

Another question that comes up is what should the altar actually BE? A shelf? A table? One of those tiny altar tables from the occult shop? Ideally, you should use anything that works for the space you have and the items you want to put on it, and that may be a small designated altar table, or a shelf, or a coffee table or a cabinet.

You can google altar tables and find some really cool results. A lot of witches appreciate the size of them, because they're generally kind of small and they are on very low legs. This makes them super portable, plus they're easy to pick up and move or put away, which is handy if you don't have a space to keep a permanent altar out in the room.

As I mentioned, I use a shelf for my tarot altar, my mantle for my seasonal altar, and my working altar is the top of a cabinet. I keep all my tools, crystals, candles, incense, herbs, and so forth inside the cabinet. It isn't fancy; my mother-in-law gave it to me because she found it on clearance at Home Goods, and for some reason she thought of me. So it was free to me, and it came at just the time when I really needed a new place to keep my altar. The Universe provides.

What to keep on a working altar is a whole other consideration. I'm going to go through a lot of the items traditionally found on a witch's altar or a pagan altar, but you don't have to have all these things, and you may want to add things I didn't even think of. Altars are personal, and your altar is your own.

The first item on our list is the altar cloth. The purpose of an altar cloth is just to set aside the space as consecrated. It's an act of reverence, it's a way to identify this sacred space as such. Any cloth that you designate as your altar cloth will do, the color and pattern do not matter unless you choose to specifically incorporate color correspondences, which is fully valid. I have a few different cloths that I use, although oftentimes I must admit, I don't actually use one at all. Depends on my mood.

You can use silk scarves, you could use a lace doily, you can go online and do a search for altar cloths and find some really gorgeous ones that are full of occult symbolism, some have the different moon phases, you could find one with a pentacle on it, whatever suits you. They don't need to be expensive.

Another common theme in a witchcraft altar is to represent each of the elements. Fire will typically be represented by candles, water will be a small glass or bowl of altar water, or you may choose to represent water with seashells Air may be represented by incense or feathers, and to represent earth, you may want to use a crystal or a stone, some salt, or a small plant. I've even seen a little handmade clay figure used to represent earth.

Some other traditional elements include a chalice or a vessel of some kind. This is meant to symbolize the divine feminine, it may also be used to hold ritual wine, spirits or water or other offerings. A cauldron is another traditional item kept on a working altar, this is of course going to be used to burn intentions, herbs, resins, incense, etc.

An athame, or ritual knife, is also common. The athame is masculine, it's meant to be used symbolically to direct or cut through energy, it can be used to cast a circle, or in cord cuttings or what have you. It isn't meant to be used as a proper knife for cutting herbs or anything, it really is a symbolic tool. A small ritual bell or a singing bowl is another tool you might keep on the altar. These are used to clear energy using sound, and they may be used to begin a ritual and/or to bring it to a close.

If you are working with or getting to know a deity, you may want to include something that represents them, such as a small drawing or artist's depiction, or a god or goddess figurine or a statue.

Other elements you may want to include with that would be offerings, such as herbs, flowers, fruits, wine or spirits, gems, or stones that correspond with this deity. Most deities have animals that are associated with them or that they themselves hold sacred, so small figurines of those animals may be something you'd like to include too.

And beyond that, your altar should have on it whatever is meaningful to you at a given time. If you're currently working on a manifestation, you could certainly include something that represents or supports that manifestation, whether it's a new job, a romantic partner, more money, whatever the case may be.

Arrange everything on this altar in a way that is pleasing to you, that works with the space that's available, and that feels right. You don't have to keep everything on the altar at a given time, you can rotate elements in and out as you see fit or as you're working with different goals in mind.

Sabbat or seasonal altars are really just a designated place to acknowledge and honor the turning of the wheel of the year. It's a way to mark the passing of time and to celebrate the differences in the seasons, the weather, and the symbolism associated with the witches' holidays.

And this space is definitely more focused on aesthetics, so get as ornate or as simple as you like, if and when you do decide to construct a seasonal altar. And what's really cool about a seasonal altar is that if you're in a position where you have to be careful about the outward expression of your witchcraft, well, most people aren't going to bat an eyelash at a lovely seasonal tablescape in someone's home or bedroom or office.

It's easy and inexpensive to decorate for a sabbat or for the change of seasons, and it can be really fun. I look forward to it every time I rotate my wheel of the year. I think about what I want to add or include on the altar this time. Some of my favorite pieces have been found on clearance after a season is coming to an end. And it isn't any more complicated than that.

Now, ancestor altars are typically used during Samhain, but you can also make and keep an ancestor altar at any time of year for a departed loved one who you were and are very close to, or if you've been receiving messages from an ancestor, or if you're attempting to reach out to and work with a ancestor. And in this case, this doesn't have to be its own stand-alone altar. You can absolutely make space on your working altar that's dedicated to this person if you like.

I will just say this: if you're inviting spirits to your altar in this way, you might want to find some other place to keep this altar than your bedroom. These spirits do not run on a 9-5 schedule and they do not give a lukewarm shit if you have to be up early. They will keep you up all night, they will be knocking and whispering and spooking your cats, so just bear that in mind.

And as for what to keep on an ancestor altar, we can include pictures of this person if we have them, or keepsakes that belonged to them, even letters they wrote. And we will work with this person just like with a deity, we will meditate or commune with them to discover what kind of offerings they would like. And don't be alarmed or surprised or dismayed if, in addition to flowers or foods, they ask for cigarettes and liquor.

This is not uncommon at all. Our departed loved ones are still the same people on the other side as they were here, and they miss those vices, those little guilty pleasures. So if you hope to cultivate a comfortable, working relationship, don't deny them what they ask for. It is against my own ethics to support the cigarette industry, but if my great Aunt Edna wants Marlboro 100's, that's what she gets.

We can always find altar inspiration posts online, and they're really beautiful and well-lit and precisely curated, but we really can't get hung up on recreating what someone else has created. The purpose of an altar, especially a working altar, is to be effective. Its purpose is to be used.

The things on our altars are meant to be handled, and picked up and moved. So when we construct our altars, we have to be mindful first and foremost that everything serves a purpose and is meaningful, and is placed where it is most convenient and most useful, and then worry about the aesthetic second.

The best altar in the world is the one that you feel comfortable using. If we spend all day setting everything up artistically and then are reluctant to use it because we don't want to ruin the look, then it isn't doing us any good. We aren't going to get much magick out of it. And that's the most important thing I can say about that.

CRYSTALS

C rystals are big business these days, and we witches have always hoarded stones and crystals that speak to us, so I thought we could spend a little time discussing them. We are also going to talk about different metals too, because they can also have a lot of significance and power and we shouldn't overlook them.

Stones, crystals, and metals are powerful carriers of, and tools for, earth magick. These materials sit in and under the ground, they have absorbed earth's energies for billions of years before being brought to the surface. They really do vibrate at different frequencies, as much as that is such a New Age trope, but it's actually scientifically true.

And that's how crystals are able to assist us in our magick. We have a desire, we have a goal, or an intention, and we choose a stone or a crystal with sympathetic vibrational frequencies to help us attract whatever it is that we need or want. And crystals aren't always attracting things toward them, they also radiate, so if there is some attribute we are trying to convey, like confidence, or beauty, the right crystals and stones will help us to do that as well.

But when we get a new stone or crystal, the first thing we need to do is to cleanse it, and then charge it. There are several ways to cleanse your stones. Placing them in a dish of salt is simple and effective, or you can leave them in the sun for the day, you can also use water to cleanse them, but I will reiterate the warning that I gave back in the Water Magick section:

Many crystals, gems, and metals that are NOT safe to mix with water. Obviously, many metals will corrode and rust in water, so unless you're certain that it's pure gold or stainless steel, I don't recommend submerging it.

Another way to cleanse them is to use smoke, this is one I use frequently. Light some incense or sage, and pass the stones through the smoke as it rises to get any old funky energy off of it. And then charge it. There are several ways to charge your stones as well. And the purpose of this is to get the stone or crystal ready for whatever work it is about to do.

Stones and crystals all have several properties, not just one, so for example if you have a citrine that you are going to use for some purpose, you need to tell the stone, essentially, whether it's going to be using it's abilities for abundance, or to create harmony in your marriage, or to enhance your psychic visions, you know what I mean?

So we've gotta charge it. Now, the most basic way to do this is to hold the stone in your dominant hand, and while visualizing your magical intention, pour out your own energy into the stone. And now it's ready to use. We also use the term "charging crystals" to describe what we do once we have been using a stone for a while and we feel like it's been a bit depleted. We want to recharge its magical battery. And usually this is done by either charging it under the full moon, or you can simply place your crystal with either selenite or copper overnight.

Selenite is one of the rare minerals that is self-charging. It never needs to be recharged, and it can in fact charge other stones. Selenite is pretty inexpensive and it can be found in all kinds of shapes, including bowls. The same is true for copper. If you have a copper dish, or goblet, or just a decent sized piece of copper, you can place your stones on or inside it, and the copper will recharge the stones' energy stores so that they can be used again.

The selenite and copper methods are helpful if you need to recharge your stone but you're still a few weeks out from the next full moon. And as far as knowing when your stones need to be recharged, you just have to feel it. Use your intuition.

And now I am going to go through different magical intentions and give you corresponding crystals, stones, minerals, and metals that can amplify your work.

There are a lot of metals that attract money, you can use brass, copper, tin, and of course silver and gold. Stones and crystals that are helpful are pyrite, moss agate, green calcite, green jasper, green tourmaline, malachite, jade... are you detecting the green theme here? And also bloodstone, which is green and red.

For health and healing, the metals you will want are bornite, brass, copper, iron, silver, and steel. Stones and crystals that you'll find useful are tourmaline, sunstone, aquamarine, carnelian, moldavite (if you can find it and if you can afford it, and just as a brief tangent, there are a lot of frauds out there selling fake moldavite, so if you DO buy some, make sure it's legit), salt, which is a mineral and which is very purifying, and turquoise.

For love matters, of course rose quartz is the OG. Also effective is amethyst, pink sapphire, red tourmaline or watermelon tourmaline (which I think is so gorgeous and I have been trying to talk myself into buying some, but god, I have so many crystals!), and also labradorite, lapis lazuli, coral and gold.

For overcoming obstacles (and I like to use this kind of magick because it can be combined with other kinds of magick), depending on what specifically you're trying to overcome, you'll want cat's eye, garnet, hematite, red jasper, and copper.

For amplifying psychic ability, try angelite, opal, moonstone, smoky quartz, clear quartz, jet, azurite, tiger's eye, moldavite again, iron, or silver.

For protection, try peridot, lodestone, apache tears, jade, petrified wood, peridot, onyx, obsidian, serpentine, black tourmaline, pearl, iron, lead, silver, or steel. For psychic protection specifically, try calcite, carnelian, and of course, as ALWAYS, salt. Salt, salt, salt.

For motivation, determination, and self-discipline, tanzanite, sunstone, onyx, black opal, emerald, amber, fluorite, mother-of-pearl, and silver.

But there are going to be stones that aren't identifiable at all, but which still feel important or magical. These are the stones you just find out on a trail or on a walk and decide to take home. For whatever reason, for a lot of us witches, sometimes we see a really cool stone and we just gotta bring it home. We don't even know why. But for whatever reason, those stones chose us, and we can still use them for magick.

The best way that you're going to figure out how this stone wants to be used is to sit with it for a while. And I mean set it on your nightstand for a few days or a week, and just pick it up every day and handle it for a few minutes, and see what it says to you.

I have a stone I found at the beach years ago and it likes to sit on the windowsill in my room. It soaks up all the sun's energy all day, and then it radiates out while I sleep to help me rest peacefully and keep nightmares away. This is not an especially beautiful stone, I don't even remember why I thought it needed to come home with me, but it's part of the family now, and I find it very helpful.

And all that info is well and good, but how can we best use crystals, minerals, metals, and stones? Honestly, there are all kinds of ways. Aside from using them in larger spells, there are many, many ways to incorporate them into daily life that don't require a whole ton of forethought.

It's not always practical to write up a whole spell, or put together a mojo bag or something when you're really just trying to get through the workday without strangling your boss. So let's cover those. When you're just trying to use a stone's natural abilities to confer protection, peace, abundance, general health, etcetera, there are many low-effort ways to do that.

The most obvious is of course jewelry. Choosing a stone to wear for the day is a simple and subtle way to practice your craft. Rings, earrings, necklaces, and of course, there's the time honored witch tradition of just keeping a crystal in your bra. I would love to have a dollar for every time I've come home after a long day at work to change clothes, and then had to fish around under the bed for the stone that just flew out of my bra.

Placing a stone under your pillow or under your bed, depending on your intention, is another really great way to use its power in a very passive way. The same can be said for just placing it on your altar. And of course, we should regularly be handling and changing and using our altars.

But this is reality, and sometimes life gets in the way and we just don't have the energy. During those times, placing a specific stone in a prominent power position on your altar is going to be helpful anyway.

Along those same lines, keeping a stone like green calcite in your wallet with your money is a great way to call more money in. Keeping a cat's eye or quartz in the car is very protective. Keeping a selenite on or near your tarot cards keeps their energy fresh, and keeping them with a moonstone will help you to better connect with them intuitively. A black tourmaline in your work space will discourage negativity, and in fact I keep a small vial of black salt at my desk to banish negativity as well.

Carrying a power stone like carnelian with you to a job interview can help to boost your confidence. If you have a presentation or a speech to give, kyanite is a really good stone for helping you to communicate clearly and make yourself understood to others.

There are just so many ways to use your crystals daily that don't require a lot of fuss, and when you do this, it helps you to connect with them and to attune with their energies in a really personalized way. Of course there are very complicated spells that use crystals, and you can definitely try crystal gridding if that is something that appeals to you, but while that is important and it has its place, I think that the more beneficial use of crystals is the one you use every day.

Now on the topic of crystal grids. There are a lot of established crystal grid patterns: the Metatron cube, flower of life, etcetera. The purpose of doing that is so that crystals can be used in combination, and they can be oriented in such a way as to magnify one another's energies. The basic intention of a crystal grid cloth or wooden crystal grid is to help you to orient the crystals in a formation, usually using sacred geometry, that will make it easier to achieve that.

It's a cool way to use your crystals, and it is very powerful. But it requires a lot of crystals and it is a very visual method, so I'm not going to go much deeper than that basic explanation. There are a ton of images online and YouTube tutorials that can walk you through different grids and the best combinations of crystals to use for your specific intent.

And along that vein, the shape of a crystal can be significant as well. In general, no it doesn't affect a crystal's overall attributes, but certain shapes and formations can make it easier to wield a crystal more effectively. Tumbled stones have a smoother, calmer energy, whereas raw stones are stronger and a tad more... let's not say unpredictable, but perhaps more free-spirited. Cubes are generally very grounding, spheres are excellent for scrying (hello crystal balls!), and pyramids are really good for focusing all that energy and especially for clearing blockages according to what the crystal is.

And by that I mean that an obsidian pyramid will clear blockages related to mental stress and tension for example, whereas a pyrite pyramid will help to clear emotional or intellectual blockages.

Crystal points are basically magick wands, you can wield them and direct the energy where you want it to go. Double-terminated points, which just means that both ends of the crystal are pointy, can draw energy in and then emit energy back out. So just keep in mind when you're choosing a crystal that in addition to the actual crystal or stone itself, the shape might matter depending on how you intend to use it. But again, the properties of the crystal are the properties of the crystal, no matter what shape it's in.

And my final thought on crystals is this: don't go broke buying crystals. A few crystals that you use all the time are going to be worth much more to you than a pile of crystals that you never use and can't even remember what they are. And if you're wondering if I am a huge crystal nerd, the answer is yes the hell I am. But the god's honest truth is that I constantly forget which crystal is which and I am sick of taking them to my local crystal shop to have the experts there help me to re-identify them. It's embarrassing.

MOON MAGICK

We have talked so many times about different ways to use the power of the moon, but now we are going to devote this a chapter to all the different moon phases and how we, as witches, can use those natural rhythms to enhance our spell work and our lives in general.

Now before we really get into the different phases and how we can use them, I want to preface this by saying that you can always do any spellwork any time of the month. You never need to wait on a specific moon phase to do your work. Timing your work with the moon just offers some extra mojo, that's all. And also, the power of a moon phase lingers a couple days before and afterwards, so even if you missed the exact night of a full moon, or whatever, you can still perform your work the next night and get that extra moon sauce in.

So with alllll that said, let's get lost in the big, beautiful moon.

New Moon: The first phase I want to talk about is the new moon. This is also called the dark moon, and is associated most closely with the crown and heart chakras. The crown is the seventh chakra and is what connects us with the divine, with consciousness, cosmic energy and enlightenment, spiritual illumination, knowledge and wisdom.

The heart is the fourth chakra and is associated with balance, compassion and empathy, healing and nurturing, love, affection, and relationships. So if any of these areas are lacking, consider doing some spellwork or at least some meditation or mindfulness activities during the new moon to kickstart those intentions.

If you work with deities, the Morrigan is often called the dark moon goddess. She rules battle, courage, death, destruction, empowerment, hexes, messages and omens, nightmares, power and prophecy. So if you're doing work in any of those areas, the new moon will be the right phase for you.

This is also the moon phase we look to when we are searching for wisdom, when we're doing work that requires us to look inward and be very introspective. When we want illumination in a situation or area of our lives that we are having trouble seeing clearly, when we seek hidden knowledge, and when we are working on our shadow selves, we should look to the new moon. The new moon is a good time for banishing work, but maybe surprisingly, it can also be the best moon phase for new undertakings.

The best workings for a new moon (in my completely subjective opinion) are those times when we are trying to start something brand new from scratch, something that is going to need to grow and build upon itself. Spellwork for new projects that we are beginning from the absolute ground up are going to be really well supported by this energy.

In addition, I think the new moon is the best time of month for doing the work of facing our shadow selves, of really looking at our true selves full in the face and acknowledging the things we do and the ways we think that we aren't really super proud of or that we are in denial about. You know, we can hide a lot about ourselves from the outside world, but we can hide it from ourselves too.

The new moon is an opportunity to pull those aspects of ourselves out into the light and, if not change those things, at least to confront them. The new moon assists us with beauty, beginnings, darkness and destruction, self-improvement, psychic abilities, and renewal in all its forms.

First Quarter: The first quarter moon, which is also commonly known as the waxing moon, follows a week or so after the new moon. This phase begins just as the moon cycle begins to grow and build toward the full moon again. This phase is associated with the sacral and solar plexus chakras.

The sacral chakra is the second chakra, it's associated with abundance, connections, creativity, desire, pleasure, passion, and sexuality, fertility, freedom, and motivation. So when you're trying to create new patterns in your life, this is a good moon phase for that.

The solar plexus is the third chakra, and rules authority, confidence, pride and courage, respect, personal power, sensitivity, and willpower. So we can kind of see how that blends nicely with the motivation aspect of this phase as well. When we find ourselves caught up in patterns that we want to break, or while we are working to establish new patterns, or even when we hope to do both of those things at the same time, the first quarter moon is a great time for this sort of work.

This is also a great moon phase for becoming an advocate for yourself. If you've been allowing yourself to be a doormat in a friendship, a romantic relationship, at work, with your family, now is the time to reverse the tides. Allow this moon phase to assist you in establishing boundaries and enforcing the treatment you deserve. If you're finally ready to cut off a toxic friend, let the waxing moon help you find your voice.

This is a phase of abundance, and of attraction. Not necessarily physical attraction, but rather attracting that which we want to call in for ourselves. This is a phase of increase, growth, luck, wealth, inspiration, business success and money.

Second Quarter: The second quarter moon is also called the waning moon, and this is the phase about a week following the full moon, when the moon is once again circling back to its dark, or new moon state. The waning moon rules the brow and throat chakras.

The brow is the sixth chakra, and rules clairaudience, clairvoyance, imagination, insight, psychic visions, and hidden wisdom. The throat is the fifth chakra and rules communication, creativity, inspiration, and truth.

The waning moon is perfect therefore, for spellwork associated with secrets, divination, prophecy, and spirit work. This is a great moon phase for meditating with amethyst to exercise your own psychic muscles. There are a lot of exercises to do that can help build your abilities, and the waning moon is a wonderful time to do them.

But it's also helpful with banishing, binding, reversal spells, rebirth and renewal, endings, and death magic, AND otherworld or interdimensional work. Which makes it a great phase for practicing astral travel, or connecting with spirit guides and ancestors, the fae, or for any kind of paranormal investigations.

Full Moon: The full moon gets all the attention, and it makes sense; that's arguably the most beautiful moon phase. But it is also incredibly powerful. The full moon is associated with the heart chakra, just as the new moon is, but it also rules the root chakra, which is the first, or base chakra. This is the chakra associated with manifestation, vitality, attachments, comfort, endurance, grounding, motivations, security and stability, and our needs.

The full moon is also associated with the goddess Selene, although she is a moon goddess in general, not only in the full moon phase. But approaching her during the full moon is common. Selene is the goddess of cycles, calm and tranquility, enchantment, moon magic, nightmares and sleep, and youth and beauty.

The full moon itself rules wisdom, protection, particularly for children and pregnant women, illumination, creativity, divination work, psychic abilities in all their forms, accomplishments, energy, growth, healing, emotions, and intuition. So if you're trying to get insight on an issue that's been plaguing you and you aren't sure maybe what the truth of the matter is, meditating on it during the full moon is going to give you a lot of clarification.

The full moon is a great tool for charging crystals, tarot decks, amulets, talismans, and of course for making moon water. Full moon rituals are very common for witches who are setting intentions for an entire moon cycle, meaning they've worked some sort of spell or manifestation, and they are setting it in motion at the full moon with the purpose of using the magick of an entire 28 day cycle to energize it. Full moon rituals are also just a good way to bathe yourself in the power and energy of the moon in its fullest form.

Sex magick is really powerful during the full moon as well, so consider that if your intent needs a super-charged kickstart, combining sex magick and the full moon will get strong, undeniable results.

If you're really trying to create a laser focus for your spellwork this year, you may use the monthly full moon associations to target specific spellwork goals. For example, the January full moon is associated with beginnings (obviously), healing, and money work.

February's moon is great for astral work, fertility and empowerment. March will be especially helpful for prosperity and success. April for fertility and growth. May for divination, love and enchantment. June is for marriage and relationship magic. Juy is a good moon for dream work and renewal of purpose.

August is the moon for abundance and prophecy work. September will be helpful for protection magic, especially of the home and family. October of course will be excellent for ancestor work, November for cooperation, healing and hope, and December for peace, prosperity, and strength.

There are other lunar events not included on this list, for example the blue moon. Now, there are differing definitions of what makes a blue moon. The most frequent use of this term is applied anytime there are two full moons in the same calendar month, and using this definition, the second full moon is commonly called a blue moon. This happens fairly regularly and isn't all that rare.

But before that usage, blue moons were defined as happening whenever there were 13 full moons in a calendar year instead of 12. So rather than three full moons per season, one season would have four full moons. This only happens every 2 or 3 years, and so it is pretty rare. The power of a blue moon is best used for goals, goal setting and goal achieving.

Sun Magick: Now, we can't talk about the moon without giving the sun a little bit of a shout out. I feel like, unfortunately, the sun just does not get the recognition it deserves when it comes to witchcraft. And that's not anyone's fault, it's just that witchcraft is something that tends to be done in darkness, indoors, or outside at night. The moon is a powerful source of energy for witches, but the sun is no less powerful.

Leos are ruled by the sun, so if you're a Leo, and you find yourself having a little trouble connecting to the moon, or using the moon in your magic, then definitely try using the power of the sun. I've mentioned before that my daughter was lamenting once that she just wasn't feeling the moon, like she just couldn't quite connect like she thought that she should. But my daughter is a big old Leo, and once she stopped fighting that aspect of herself, things felt a little more natural.

She started charging her crystals and cards in the sunlight, and stopped worrying so much about using the correct moon phase for her work. Eventually, she found a balance, but there was, initially at least, a little bit of a disconnect, and I truly think it was just due to the power that she personally draws from the sun.

If you find yourself not quite coming alive when the sun goes down, then don't fight that inclination. The sun is a powerful source of strength, and we all owe our very lives to it. Do your spells in the sunlight, meditate in the sunlight, charge your crystals in the sun, just go for it.

WORKING WITH
DEITIES

I f you're interested in deity work, there are some things to consider. A lot of witches won't necessarily work with a certain god or goddess by name, but they may call upon the god or goddess archetype. We see this a lot with Wiccans, of course, but many times the work that we may be doing doesn't necessarily merit or require the intervention of a specific deity, but will be amplified by the invocation of THE god, or THE goddess, as an archetype.

So for example if you're doing some shadow work for yourself and trying to embrace the divine feminine more, or conversely, maybe you're trying to lean into your more masculine traits, you may call upon the goddess or the god just as an embodiment of those qualities. And for the record, when we work with the maiden, mother, or crone archetypes, we are doing the same thing. We are working with the representative prototype of an ideal.

And of course, when we say god, goddess, divine feminine, etc, it bears mentioning that no matter who we are or what bodies we are in, we all embody feminine and masculine qualities to differing degrees. So I'm not trying to paint everyone with a broad brush when we talk about god, goddess, masculine, feminine, and none of those descriptors carries more weight or value than another.

It is just a way of cataloging and simplifying aspects to make them easier to understand and connect with.

Now before you just start invoking any deity, it is a good idea to learn as much as you can about this entity. Try to understand their basic history, the more prominent myths and traditions associated with them, learn what correspondences they may have, so that when you do approach them, you will be able to present a suitable offering for them. And once you've done whatever working you had in mind with this deity, don't forget to thank them afterward.

Once you've got a deity's attention, you want to be sure you remain on good terms.

Working with deities takes time and planning, especially the first time you work with them. This isn't something to try the day before you start your spell. This could take weeks of planning. Save this kind of work for your larger spells. Once you've done your homework and learned all you can, then create a space for this entity on your altar for the duration of the spell, and even for some time afterwards. Keep flowers, herbs, crystals, candles, runes, or incense that are significant to this deity. Even pictures or a small statuette of them can go a long way toward gaining their favor. Meditate with them for some time. Develop a relationship before you go asking for favors.

I suggest that if you are curious about working with a particular entity, that you take your time. And I do not recommend that you jump from one deity to another. You may find it beneficial to work with one particular deity for months at a time.

I personally have found that I tend to have seasons where I will feel called to work with one deity. Not necessarily for spells or anything, but just to learn about them, and learn from them, sort of an apprenticeship, I suppose. And it seems as though certain deities will come to me at different times or phases in my life, and beyond any magick that we may or may not do together, it's the knowledge and the wisdom that comes from those relationships that I take with me.

So. Once that relationship is established and you've done a bit of work with them and you feel that connection, it will be easier going forward to work with them again. It won't require quite so much effort on the front end, but you will still want to approach them with respect and they will still want those tributes. Gods and goddesses love to be remembered, they love to be honored, and they don't tolerate disrespect. So just keep all that in mind.

There are a lot of deities that I don't work with at all and likely never will, because they aren't a part of my heritage or traditions, and it would feel disingenuous to ask them for assistance. But, there are some that I do work with, like Aphrodite for example. I am not Greek, but Greek and Roman theology have become so universal precisely because they are so accessible, that I don't feel like some kind of an interloper when I call upon her.

So I will go through a few deities that I feel are pretty approachable and who I do occasionally work with and just talk briefly about their correspondences and some of the intentions and issues they may be most helpful with. Starting with Aphrodite.

Aphrodite is the Greek goddess of love, sex, sensuality, and passion, but also fidelity, marriage, fertility, and childbirth. She is associated with apples and walnuts, so those make excellent offerings, and you would do well to place roses, daisies, or violets on her altar. Salt, pearls, and copper are associated with Aphrodite, and cinnamon or myrrh incense would be my suggestions. When you've done the work of reaching out to her and establishing a relationship, look for signs in the form of the repeating number 1, and also doves, deer, goats, and seagulls.

Athena, goddess of war, is another Greek deity I find approachable. She isn't only the goddess of war, though, she can also be called upon when you're trying to establish peace in a troubled relationship. She is a guardian, she confers strength, harmony, healing, and justice. She will appreciate apples again, and olives on her altar. Yellow candles will please her, as will fir or maple incense. Look for repeating sixes or sevens as a sign from her, as well as owls, ravens, snakes, or horses.

Brigid is a Celtic triple goddess, and her issues and strengths include communication, healing, marriage, pregnancy, money, poetry, and knowledge. Place dandelions and blackberries on her altar, along with blue candles, azurite or peridot crystals, and cedar incense. Look for signs in the form of bears, swans, or oak trees.

Demeter, especially if you're a gardener, is another Greek goddess for you. She is the goddess of grain and the fruitfulness of the earth. She is a wonderful goddess to build and maintain an altar for in your garden itself. She is also a good deity to approach in matters of abundance, manifestation, grounding, changes and cycles, and grief.

On her altar, or even directly in your garden, keeping poppies, roses or sunflowers in her honor are appreciated, placing barley, corn or wheat on her altar is smart, along with burning myrrh incense. And then the signs she may send could include cats, doves, and honeybees. I love Demeter, she is such a vibe.

Dionysus is the first god on our list. He is the god of wine, pleasure, and civilization. This is my mom's favorite deity. She has the most beautiful little statuette of him. You may approach Dionysus in matters of business, happiness, sex magic, creativity, and travel. When building his altar, think about wine (of course) apples, laurels, grapes, and ivy. Amethyst and/or silver will be at home on that altar as well, and you will want to look for signs such as the repeating number 5, or maybe tigers, lambs, griffins, or the horse.

Green Man is another male entity, although this one isn't a god per se. The Green Man is a pagan spirit of abundance, agriculture, and male fertility and sexuality, so there may be a time when you will want to approach him. His primary symbol is the oak, so definitely pile some acorns on that altar.

Hekate is one of the main goddesses that witches will call upon, as she is quite literally the goddess of witchcraft. She, like the Morrigan, is another triple goddess. She is a crossroads goddess, and this will be the best place to place your petitions, although it's still a good idea to keep a place for her on your altar.

I have worked very successfully with Hekate in the past. Her origins are also Greek, and she will be a powerful ally in matters of business, destruction, empowerment and influence, karma, magic, particularly, defensive magic, moon magic, and baneful magic, and she is also influential in shamanic or healing work.

To win her favor, place pearls, moonstone, quartz or sapphire on her altar, feverfew and lavender flowers, and burn myrrh incense. Look for signs such as the numbers 3 or 9, and animal totems like rabbits, owls, and especially dogs.

The Morrigan is another Celtic goddess, but she just isn't someone you can give a concise explanation for. She is so complex and her lore is so rich. She is a triple goddess, a goddess of war, battle, death, destruction, vengeance, and hexes, but she is also a goddess of courage, defense, empowerment, messages and omens, prophecy, protection, and shamanic work. She IS the goddess of witches.

So absolutely by all means, if you feel called to work with her, please do. But, and this goes for every deity I have listed already, please learn as much as you can before you approach her. Once you have her attention, you'd better be ready for the ride.

But I'm not trying to make anyone nervous. There are so many deities I didn't get to, of course Selene the moon goddess is very special, Vesta is a powerful goddess in family and domestic magic, Lugh the sun god is another Celtic deity, and in fact he's who we celebrate at Lughnasadh.

There are gods for every issue. And it can be so enriching to work with them and see how much extra sauce they can bring to your magic. And that's really the point of this. Yes, you can do all kinds of amazing magick on your own, and 95% percent of the time, I do magick solo. But that 5% is just so spicy.

DIVINATION

All that divination is, really, is the practice of seeking knowledge of the future or the unknown by supernatural means. This means different things to different witches, perhaps for you it means tarot and oracle cards, or runes, pendulums, ouija boards, scrying, astrology, reading tea leaves, reading palms, numerology, or even just straight up reading omens in the events that happen in your life. And it really doesn't end there.

Now, my personal favorite method of divination is tarot, and we will get deep into it in the next chapter, but this is just a primer. I know not every witch uses tarot cards, but a lot of us do and I think most of us are at least aware of tarot, if not familiar with it. There are almost as many different kinds of tarot decks as there are different kinds of witches, so it's easy these days to find a deck that speaks to you. And here I must debunk a common misconception that I've heard so many times, this false idea that you're not supposed to buy your own tarot cards. There's an old witch's tale that started somewhere along the way that you're supposed to wait for someone else to buy tarot cards for you.

This is pseudo-mysticism bullshit. You absolutely do not have to wait for someone else to buy you a tarot deck, and in fact I much prefer to buy my own decks because I can be assured that it's a deck that I like and that resonates with me. So go to your local occult shop and handle the decks, or go online and look at the many hundreds, if not thousands, of tarot decks in all shapes, sizes, price points, and artistic mediums.

Find yourself a deck that feels good in your hands and that you're intuitively able to connect with. On the other hand, if someone does buy tarot cards for you, well that's a lovely gesture, but unnecessary for the purposes of being able to use them effectively. It just doesn't matter who buys the cards.

And here's a fun fact: if for whatever reason you're in a position where you want to do tarot, but you're unable to, perhaps you're a younger witch living at home and your family or partner disapproves of it, or even if you're unable to afford them, or you're not quite ready to make the commitment of buying them, you can 100 percent use a regular deck of cards.

There won't be any major arcana cards in the deck, but the suits of a regular deck of cards correspond to the suits in a tarot deck and you can use them to do some really great readings.

There are differences of opinion on which card suit equates to which tarot suit, but the general consensus is that the hearts are represented by the cups in tarot, the diamonds are represented by the wands, the spades are swords, and the clubs are pentacles. I personally swap those around a little bit when I read playing cards, but again there is really not one absolute correct opinion on which suit is what. It's really up to the individual witch to decide how to read them.

Another option to physical tarot cards if that is a barrier for you is a tarot app. There are several, many of them are totally free, and they're discreet.

I like tarot a lot. I pull a card every single day because I feel like it helps me to be ready for whatever may pop up, or at least I'll be able to keep my eyes open for some kind of opportunity that may present itself. If I pull the King of Cups reversed, I'll just try to stay aware that emotions may be running high that day, and I will make more of an effort to be understanding and not jump headfirst into an unnecessary argument or whatever.

If there's a larger issue going on in my life, or if I feel like I'm at a crossroads and maybe there's some kind of decision coming up, I'll do a larger spread to help tease out the pros and cons of a situation, or to give me a more objective view of a situation. The thing about tarot cards is that they are there to give you the straight shit. Tarot cards are not there to coddle you and tell you what you want to hear. But I've gone on far too long already, so I'll leave it here until the next chapter.

Oracle cards are similar to tarot in that they will have some sort of themed artwork, and again there are hundreds upon hundreds of different decks. They're not the same as tarot though. Tarot decks almost always have 78 cards, with minor and major arcana. The meanings of each card will be similar, if not identical, across each deck.

Oracle cards, on the other hand, have no set rules about what kind of cards are going to be in the deck or what each card may mean. For example, I have a botanical oracle deck wherein each plant has a message that it conveys, and I have an animal oracle deck where each animal brings a different lesson, but there is no crossover whatsoever in the messaging. They are completely unrelated.

Oracle decks are more of a tool for self-reflection and they will tend to offer the reader some aspect of their lives or their outlook to meditate on.

Oracle decks are also generally a little more straightforward and easy to read, and they're usually a bit more gentle in the way they will convey a message. If you're doing a love reading with tarot and you pull the three of hearts and the seven of swords, tarot is basically telling you that this person is going to rip your heart out and pour salt on the wound.

But an oracle deck will deliver this message much more gently. The messaging tends to be a bit more focused on positivity and aspiration, self-care, and reflection. They can be a great tool to use alongside tarot too, especially if you're having difficulty trying to figure out the meaning of a tarot spread. Sometimes it can be helpful to pull an oracle card to shine a little more light on what tarot may be trying to tell you.

Next on the list is runes. Runes are so cool. They're most commonly made of stone, but also crystal, bone, and wood as well. You can make your own runes easily and at no cost to you by simply finding some small stones that are similar in size and drawing or craving the symbols onto them. Runes are usually of the Elder Futhark variety (which you can Google to see what they look like and what each symbol means), but you can certainly add your own designs as well which will have more personal meaning to you.

The way that runes work is much like any other divination method. You meditate on a question or a situation until you feel like your focus is very clear, and then you cast your stones. Some folks like to look at the way the runes are grouped to determine the message. For example if you're trying to start a family and the rune representing fertility is next to or touching the rune which denotes delays, you may expect some difficulties in becoming pregnant.

Other ways to interpret the meaning is that the runes in the center of the cast are the more pressing issues that demand your attention, while the runes on the edges of the grouping are less immediate. Runes which are flipped upside down are interpreted to mean that they're not important at the moment, or they can be interpreted to mean that instead of a literal or physical interpretation, the message is more spiritual. Other readers interpret these upside down runes to mean that the matter isn't current, but will pop up later on, so you'll need to watch out for it.

The point is, when you start reading runes, you'll most likely stick closely to what you see online or in your rune guidebook, if your set comes with one. But as you become more experienced, you're going to start relying more on your own interpretations and understandings. And frankly, that's the whole theme of divination.

Each of our minds and spirits is different, and we are all going to read omens differently. This is normal and it's to be expected, but most importantly, this is the way it's supposed to be. There is no one size fits all way to practice divination or any other form of witchcraft.

Pendulums are a fun one, and they can easily be combined with other forms of divination. A pendulum is just some kind of object suspended on a string, a ribbon or a chain. Pendulums can be made of crystal or metal, you can use a ring or a pendant on a necklace chain, you can use an acorn, a hagstone, basically anything you like. Anything that is meaningful to you. And you just have to get in touch with your pendulum and figure out how it wants to communicate with you.

For yes or no questions for example, simply ask the pendulum a question to which you already know the answer. So I might ask my pendulum, Am I 25 years old? My personal pendulum is going to swing from left to right, and that is how my pendulum tells me 'Nice try Eli, you are not 25'. If I then ask my pendulum, is my dog's name John? My pendulum swings forward and backward, which is how my pendulum indicates YES. Your results may be different, but this is why you have to ask your pendulum questions like this, so you will know what it is indicating and the way that it communicates.

You can also buy or make a pendulum board or cloth, which is simply a cloth or board printed or engraved with areas that indicate yes, no or maybe. The idea is that your pendulum will swing towards the correct answer. But I find that this isn't really necessary. If you're in good communication with your pendulum, you'll be able to understand those simple answers easily.

But, there are pendulum boards that feature the entire alphabet so that you can get more detailed answers. It takes a lot longer, because the pendulum has to spell everything out by swinging towards each letter it wants to indicate individually, but sometimes, that's what you need.

You can also use a pendulum in combination with tarot cards. For this you will fan all your tarot cards out, face down so that you don't unintentionally interfere with the results, and focus on your question. Steady your pendulum and slowly hover it across the spread. Once your pendulum is over the card that answers your question, your pendulum will start to swing or spin, or otherwise get your attention, and you'll pull the card and get your answer.

Scrying is a little more arcane as a divination method, and it's a lot more open to individual interpretation. There are a lot of different ways to scry, you can use smoke, fire, running water, you can gaze into a dark mirror, which is a very popular method with witches, and of course we can't talk about scrying without mentioning gazing into a crystal ball. The basic method is to find a quiet place to work with whichever media you plan to use for your scrying session and center yourself.

Once your mind is quiet, you can gaze deeply into the flame or smoke or water or what have you, and let your mind just receive whatever messages may come to you. If you're using a mirror or a crystal, I recommend doing your scrying in a dark room by the light of a candle to get better results.

If you like, you can have a pen and paper nearby to write down your impressions, but if you find that too distracting or if it takes you out of the moment, you can just wait until you're done with your session and write things down afterward.

All kinds of images, words, phrases, scenarios, and memories may come to you while you're scrying, it's a lot like meditation. You may find that your mind wanders, and if that happens, don't get frustrated. Just acknowledge those thoughts and let them go.

If you find an especially intrusive thought keeps coming to mind or, what happens to me a lot, is that something will come to mind that I need to remember or to do, and my mind won't stop dredging it up, and THAT'S why I keep a pen and paper nearby. I just make a note, and go back to scrying. Don't make judgements about those thoughts, don't get frustrated, just allow them to come and then go.

Once you feel like your session has come to an end, spend some time with your notes and see what you can make of the information that may have come through. Often, you'll feel like none of it makes any sense, but that's ok. Just look the information over anyway. Within a few days or a week, you may find that a lot of the images that presented themselves to you start to make sense in one way or another.

When those affirmations come through, make note of that too. It's nice to be able to go back to those old readings and see what kind of predictions you were able to make.

Palm reading and tea leaf reading, or tasseomancy, are two areas that I have really only ever dabbled in. Well, I've more than dabbled, but still I don't really feel super comfortable speaking with any degree of authority there, but what I like about these methods is that they don't require any special equipment and they're inexpensive to learn.

All it really costs you is time and effort. But when you're learning something new that you find interesting, the fun is in the learning. Another thing I like about these methods is that they're open to your personal interpretation. Once you've learned the basics of these methods, you can really take it from there and create your own codes and meanings for what you see.

Astrology and numerology are two really serious disciplines, and they're not going to get a very good summary from the likes of me in a short section of a brief chapter. All I can really say about them is that there are a lot of resources to get you started in the way of books, videos, websites, and so on. If those are methods that pique your interest, you can really divine a lot of valuable information this way.

The thing about divination is to just do it. Even the act of trying to divine information will begin to open up your abilities, and those intuitive feelings will start to present themselves even when you're not necessarily using a divination method. And you'll start building your confidence in your abilities and really step into your destiny as an all-powerful, all-knowing badass.

TAROT

I freaking love tarot. Did I mention that yet? Tarot is one of my favorite tools for witchcraft, and it's without a doubt the tool I use most often. Not every witch uses tarot, and not every one who uses tarot is a witch, and I get that and it's valid. But this chapter is for the witches who do, or at least for the witches who would like to.

One complaint that I do frequently hear is that tarot seems intimidating. My own mother has had trouble connecting with tarot, because it really can be a bit overwhelming. The typical tarot deck has 78 cards, each with unique meanings and significance. Tarot relies on a lot of symbolism, numerology, and intuition, so it really can feel like... a lot. But it doesn't have to be that way, so let's break it down a bit. Demystify it. It ain't that serious.

The origins of tarot are found in Italy beginning in the 1400's. Tarot was originally just a card game, but over time, it sort of morphed and evolved and became what we know today as a divination tool. Sometimes people are caught by surprise to find out that tarot began as just a game, but that really shouldn't surprise us. Ouija boards are produced by the same company that makes Candy Land, for crying out loud. Like everything else in witchcraft, anything can be a tool; it just depends on how we use it.

Now, if you don't really want to learn tarot, or if you're not really sure if you want to bother, something that can be helpful to at least dip a toe in the tarot waters before you spend money or time that you aren't sure if you want to invest yet, is to try a tarot app. You know I love a free app. My current favorite is called Golden Thread tarot. I just like the minimalist look of the app, but there really are a lot of apps to choose from. As always, this is NOT a paid endorsement.

These apps will have a 'card a day' function, where you'll open the app and it will pull a card for you and give you the meaning. It may have other functions as well, but the point is to get to know the cards and get a feel for tarot before you spend any money. These apps are also helpful if you're not in a living situation where it would be safe to have physical tarot cards lying around. Everyone's lives are different, and we are all under different constraints, and sometimes it isn't possible to be as open about things like tarot. People love to have opinions about what other people do.

That's okay; there's always a workaround.

Most tarot decks, as we mentioned, have 78 cards. And I'm going to be mostly using the Ryder Waite cards as a reference just because it's so iconic. There are four different suits, usually cups, pentacles, swords, and wands, although the suits vary a bit across different decks. There are 14 cards of each suit, making 56 minor arcana cards. The minor arcana cards are numbered ace, 2, 3, 4 and so on up to ten, and then there's the page, the knight, queen and king. The four suits correspond with the elements, and also with the signs of the zodiac. Which makes it a little easier sometimes to figure out what a particular card might be trying to tell us.

So for example, the swords correspond with the element of air, and the air signs are Libra, Gemini, and Aquarius. And of course air is also associated with reason, decision-making, and communication.

The suit of cups is associated with water, and therefore with Cancer, Scorpio, and Pisces. Cups are associated with emotions, intuition, and relationships.

Wands are the fire cards, corresponding with Leo, Aries, and Sagittarius, and also with creativity, energy, and passion.

And finally the suit of pentacles is associated with earth. This corresponds with Taurus, Virgo, and Capricorn. Pentacles will show up in a reading related to money, careers, and your physical health. And so anytime you draw a card, if you're having trouble connecting with the meaning, you can always ask yourself, "what do I know about the zodiac element that this suit represents?" to at least give yourself a starting point.

When we're getting to know the minor arcana cards, it can be tricky and really just overwhelming to try and memorize 56 different card meanings. But, in addition to knowing the elements that a suit represents, it can also help to just get familiar with what the different numbers represent. So if you've drawn the Ace of Pentacles, you may not remember exactly what that card means, but if you can remember that Pentacles are the earth suit, and they represent finance, careers, or health, and if you know that Aces represent potential, you can work out that the Ace of Pentacles may be alerting you to the possibility of some sort of material prosperity or manifestation, or even a new job.

So, in the minor arcana, Aces represent potential and new opportunity. Twos represent duality or balance. Threes represent communication and cooperation, and also sometimes they will represent groups of people. Fours represent stability and structure. Fives represent instability and often conflicts. Sixes represent growth. Sevens represent knowledge and faith. Eights represent change, and also mastery or accomplishment.

Nines mean something is coming to fruition, and tens represent completion, or something coming to an end.

The face cards, the page, knight, queen and king, have their own meanings. The face cards may represent specific people that you know, or they may represent concepts. So the page may be a person you know who is at the beginning of a journey or a new phase, someone with fresh energy. If you pull a page of swords, this may represent your kid who's about to start college, for example. Or, because the swords are associated with air signs, that card might also represent a young person who is an air sign that you may know. But it may not represent someone else at all; it could represent a concept, as I mentioned. In tarot, the page is a messenger. So the page of swords in a reading may be bringing you a message that you're about to experience a change in your way of thinking or communicating.

The knight card is always on a mission. He isn't the page; he's not at the beginning of a journey. When he appears in a reading, something is already set in motion. The knight is goal-oriented, he is here to make things happen. So when we see him, we need to be ready for whatever is coming. Because the knight is going to make things happen whether we are ready or not, and not necessarily in the most diplomatic way, so keep that in mind. The knight is kind of a blunt instrument.

The knight of swords might represent an important conversation that you maybe weren't ready to have yet because you're worried things may get heated and you might say something you regret. It might also represent a person you know who is like that; someone who just kind of says whatever is on their mind. Knight of wands is passionate and energetic and adventurous, the knight of cups is very charming and romantic, this could represent a love interest you may have. The knight of pentacles is very efficient and dependable, but he may also represent being stuck in a rut, you know, just feeling like you're stuck in a routine.

The queens represent the feminine aspects of a suit, but that doesn't mean she always represents a woman in a reading. Anyone you may know who embodies the feminine aspects of a suit may be represented when you see this card in a reading.

It may also be encouraging you to embody those qualities when you're doing a reading for yourself. So the queen of swords is very quick-thinking and perceptive. Queen of wands is vibrant and positive and creative, the queen of cups is incredibly intuitive and compassionate, and the queen of pentacles is really motherly and down to earth.

The king represents the male aspects of a suit. And so we have the king of swords who is very intellectual, but can also be a little condescending. We have the king of wands who is a visionary, he is also very entrepreneurial. The king of cups is very much in control of his emotions, but on the other hand he can sometimes have trouble expressing his emotions.

And then there's the king of pentacles who is very self-disciplined but can sometimes be too controlling. So anytime you see a face card (they're also called court cards), consider the qualities this card represents and ask yourself if this is something you need to embody more, or if a particular face card seems to remind you of someone you know, perhaps the deck is giving you a message about that person.

So without ever looking at an actual tarot card, if we have this basic information down, we can understand at least to an extent what a particular card is trying to tell us. So you could randomly pull the five of pentacles. If I know that pentacles represent money, or physical health or my career, and I know that fives indicate adversity or instability, even if that's all I know, I can get some idea what this card is trying to tell me.

Depending on what's going on in my life, using only that information, I might consider this a warning to stop spending so much money. Maybe it helps me realize that I better stop slacking at work and showing up late, or if I have been having a nagging health issue that I've been ignoring, this might be the sign for me to make an appointment with my doctor and get checked out. And we can deduce all of that, without even looking at the imagery on the cards themselves. Once we add that to the equation, we can really start to get a deeper understanding of what the cards may mean.

The 22 major arcana cards, which are also called trump cards, have their own thing going on. With the minor cards, the imagery can be useful sometimes, but because we can rely on the numbers, the suits, and the elements to give us clues, we aren't totally dependent on the imagery. But with the major arcana cards, it is all about the imagery.

So the first card, which is actually the zero card, is the Fool. He is a young man standing on the edge of a cliff, he has his little dog with him, and he's got a little bundle full of probably food and a change of clothes. He is very obviously starting a journey. He represents new beginnings and also taking a leap of faith. It's a very optimistic card.

The number one card is the Magician. His right hand is pointing toward the sky; his left hand is pointing down to earth. As above, so below. He is standing at a table, and there's a cup, a pentacle, a wand, and a sword laid out, and there's an infinity symbol above his head. This card says that we have everything we need to create the reality that we want. This is a card of power, action, and manifestation.

The high priestess is card number two, she symbolizes mystery and intuition, and also sacred knowledge. Card three is the Empress and she represents nurturing and abundance. When I think of the Empress, she is always the quintessential mother. The very best qualities of what that means.

And the Emperor therefore is the quintessential father, he

represents the very best of masculinity, and structure and stability. The Emperor is also representative of Aries. Again, these cards don't necessarily only refer to men or women, just those qualities, the archetypes.

Card five is the Hierophant, also called the Pope. This is the card of Taurus. He is the masculine counterpart to the High Priestess. So he represents traditions, conformity, and religious beliefs. But he can also just represent a teacher or an instructor. If you've been trying your hand at a new hobby or something but you're becoming discouraged, drawing the hierophant may just be a cue that you should take a proper class, or join an online community.

The Lovers card is number six, this is the card of Gemini, and that's pretty straightforward. It represents love, a union, or your romantic partnership.

Card seven is the Chariot, this is the card of Cancer. This card tells us to grab the reins and take control. This card encourages willpower and forward momentum. Card number eight is Strength, and represents exactly that; strength and courage. It also represents Leos specifically. There's a big ass lion on it. So consider both of those possible meanings.

Card nine is the Hermit. This card represents Virgo, and this card encourages us to be introspective, and to step back from the rush and the hustle.

True story, the last time I drew the Hermit I was so annoyed because I had a lot going on at the time and I couldn't really afford to pull back. And then later that day I tested positive for Covid. So the cards were basically telling me, you better clear that calendar because you aren't doing a damn thing for a while. My decks are so sassy.

Anyway, card 10 is the Wheel of Fortune. This is a messenger of karma, and destiny and it's kind of letting us know that however things have been going recently, they're about to change. What goes up, must come down, what has been down, will come up.

Card 11 is Justice. This is self explanatory, if there's some shadiness that's been going on, it's about to come to light. If you have a pressing legal issue, it's about to be resolved. This card also represents Libras, so it may be an indicator that there's a Libra in your life who needs attention.

Card 12 is the Hanged Man, and he represents surrender, or sacrifice, or seeing things from a different perspective.

Card 13 is the Death card, this is the Scorpio card, and this is the one that freaks new tarot readers out. But it isn't really a harbinger of literal death. I mean, not usually.

Death signifies the end of a cycle, or a significant transition in your life. Card 14 is Temperance, this is the Sagittarius card. This card tells us to find balance, purpose, and to have patience.

Card 15 is the Devil. This is the card of Capricorn. This card represents addiction, or vice, or bondage of some kind. If you're in a toxic relationship with a person, or with a substance, or even if you've been doing too much of something that is taking focus away from what's important in your life, the Devil card will appear to set you straight.

The Tower card represents the Tower of Babel, which according to the bible, reached to the heavens so that man could dwell with god, until god blew the shit out of the tower and punished the people for their hubris. This card warns us that a house of cards is going to come crashing down. Everything is going to come to a grinding halt and we are about to be humbled. This card warns of disaster and upheaval.

Card 17 is the Star, this is the remedy to the Tower. It represents hope and renewal. The Star is also the card of Aquarius.

Then we have the Moon, this is the card of the moody, broody

Pisces. This is the card of illusion, subconscious fears, but also intuition. The Sun card is the anti-Moon card. This is always a message of hope and positivity, and warmth.

The number 20 card is Judgment, and again, it is exactly what it claims to be. This card promises absolution for better or worse. And finally the 21 card is the World. This card represents the completion of a cycle, and great accomplishment. It also, in a very literal sense, represents travel.

Now, the minor cards usually indicate something we need to know now. The messages are shorter-term. On the other hand, when we pull the major cards, we can be assured that the message is a little farther reaching and longer lasting.

I pull a tarot card every single day, first thing in the morning, rain or shine, no matter what's going on or how I'm feeling. I do this so that I can have more information about my day. It's just nice to have a heads up if there's something I need to be looking out for.

So if I draw the five of swords, I'll be ready to watch for someone who may be trying to get away with something. If I draw the six of cups, I'll call my sister and see how she's doing. Sometimes I'll draw a card that tells me how I need to approach things. So if I pull the Queen of Pentacles, I might be extra conscientious of how I interact with my kids.

But I always pull that card. And I jot it down too. I have a planner and I always make a note of what card I've drawn because sometimes you'll pull the same card over and over, and it helps to recognize patterns. And that's really the best way, at least in my opinion, to get familiar with those meanings and to start to develop a relationship with your deck. Tarot is so useful for giving us a guidepost, or a heads-up, and I really would love for more people to use it

Sometimes, I'll do a three card spread if there are events going on in my life that I'd like clarity about, or if I have a big decision to make, if I'm worried about someone that I know, or if someone is being a pain in my ass and I want to know to what extent this person is going to cause issues for me.

The three card spread is super helpful. A quick internet search for three card spreads will give you hundreds of results for different kinds of spreads for every question or situation that you may have.

And of course there are larger spreads you can do, but for our purposes, when we are just trying to get familiar and comfortable with the cards, this is a good jumping off point. A lot of witches have tarot decks that are just collecting dust, and I hate to think of anyone letting such a wonderful tool just sit on a shelf.

Tarot can give us so much insight and so much knowledge. And I know that there are a lot of cards, but once we strip away all the mystery and just focus on what the cards are telling us, we can get a lot of information out of it. It's such a valuable practice.

SHADOW WORK

Our final topic is Shadow Work, and I've saved it for last for a reason. This is not cute work, it isn't fun, but it is probably the most important work that a witch does. This is the work that is going to help us resist sliding back into the old patterns that no longer serve us. I'm not alone when I say that Shadow Work isn't my favorite topic. Not because it isn't important. Not because it doesn't help me to grow and evolve as a witch and as a human being.

The reason I have put it off is simply because it is uncomfortable to confront these things and I am a classic avoider. It's one of my shadows. Doing shadow work truly is, in essence, removing the bandages that cover our emotional wounds and seeing if they've healed into scars that simply remind us of those old injuries, or if they've become infected. Have we allowed those injuries to quietly fester and to infect other aspects of our lives?

The term Shadow Work has become ubiquitous in witchcraft circles, but it's actually a concept that comes from Jungian psychology. Carl Jung was a Swiss psychologist and psychoanalyst. Although he was greatly influenced by Freud at the outset of his work, the two men eventually had a falling out and Jung deviated a great deal from Freud's work, and thank the gods for that.

Jung went on to do some fascinating work and I recommend any and everyone to read about some of the concepts he pioneered because he was a visionary. Not everything is going to ring true for everyone, but he truly was a forward thinker and it is remarkable how revolutionary his work really was, especially for the time.

So this next bit is going to be a super condensed crash course in Jungian psychology so we can have the tiniest bit of a foundation before we get into the meat of the matter. Jung identified numerous archetypes in the collective human psyche, which he defined as images or symbols or concepts that come from the collective unconscious.

These archetypes have universal meanings across cultures and show up in dreams, they will show up in a culture's literature, or art or even the predominant religion within a culture. He explained that the reason all these recurring themes keep showing up across cultures who may have had no historical interaction is because they have emerged from archetypes shared by the whole human race.

Jung identified many, many archetypes among individuals, but focused on four which he asserts are present in each and every one of us. These archetypes are the Self, the Persona, the Shadow and the Anima/Animus.

The Persona is the mask we wear when we face the public. This is the role we play when we perform as ourselves. The Anima/Animus refers to the unconscious masculine aspects that reside in women (this is the Animus) or the unconscious feminine aspects that reside within men (this is the Anima).

The Shadow represents the animalistic, base aspect of ourselves. It is the source of both our creative and destructive energies. And then the Self is the final archetype. This is the archetype that we are all aspiring to, which is a recognition and acceptance of all the archetypes that come together to make us a whole.

The Self, when it is actualized, understands and accepts all the different versions of ourselves and all the experiences that shape who we are and who we hope to become. And this is of course only possible once we examine, understand, and accept all of these archetypes within ourselves. And the most difficult archetype for each of us to reconcile is typically the Shadow.

I am not suggesting that Carl Jung got it all right or that his philosophies are one hundred percent correct and accurate. I'm just laying the foundation for the principals of Shadow work. So all that was the basic framework of the concept.

Shadow work as a practice seeks to bring to the forefront those aspects of ourselves that we repress or that we try to deny, or that we are ashamed of. And the reasons we may repress those aspects may not even be because they are so-called "bad" qualities. These may just be qualities that we were shamed for, or that we were punished for, whether it was deserved or not.

So we may be really conscientious of talking too much because we used to get teased for it, but talking too much isn't a "bad" thing. It isn't evil or wrong. But if it's something we were made to feel embarrassed of, we may, as adults, compensate for that by overanalyzing every social interaction we have trying to determine whether we are annoying everyone. Something as simple as this can lead to terrible social anxiety.

And there can be much larger consequences as well, for example if we weren't exposed to healthy expressions of anger and disagreement or even if we weren't allowed to express those feelings at all, we may compensate for that as adults by either turning every minor disagreement into a full-blown fight, or we may practice total conflict avoidance altogether. Which is something I personally have been working on for years. It's very difficult to undo.

Now, as for why shadow work has become such a major concept

in witchcraft, I believe this is because witches understand that we perform our best and most powerful magick when we don't have a shadow self in the background who may be unconsciously undermining this work with doubt, with negative self-talk, with insecurities, and with shame. If we can call these shadows forward and begin to understand them, if we can recognize where they came from, why they were created, what circumstances created them, we can get to know them and begin to heal them. We can integrate these shadows into our Self and start working with them rather than against them.

And remember, these shadows were created as a way to protect the Self. So, they aren't the enemy, they're simply a part of us that developed as a means of coping with events that shamed us, or shielding us from events that harmed us, or defending us from events that frightened us.

We can recognize and thank the Shadow for this service, and also relieve the Shadow from duty. But only if we recognize when, and how, and why it's triggered, and this requires the difficult shadow work.

One other factor of Shadow Work that Carl Jung sort of understood but not really, is ancestor work. Jung did acknowledge that humanity has an inherited consciousness.

However, he didn't really take that concept all the way to the conclusion of ancestral curses or generational curses, but understanding this and understanding that we are merely the most recent in a long line of our ancestors who were all carrying within their very DNA the scars and shadows of their own histories, is also a major part of healing the shadow.

So that's all cool and interesting, but how do we actually DO shadow work? Where do we begin? Well, first and foremost, understand that shadow work can be very distressing for people. Particularly if there are severe traumas in your past that haven't been effectively addressed with a competent professional, then probably you should start there. If you have access to a counselor or a therapist, please, please start there.

However, if you feel like this work is something that you're able to safely move through on your own, then a good way to begin is to simply start paying attention and noticing when our shadow appears. We need to pay attention to what triggers us.

What makes us feel anxious? What makes us feel angry? What makes us feel uncomfortable or ashamed? What makes us feel vulnerable?

Once we recognize certain events or circumstances or people who trigger these feelings in us, we can start to do the hard work of figuring out why these things cause us to feel the way we do.

And one way this is typically done is through journaling. Now you can buy shadow journals and they can be very helpful for walking a person through the process, but there are plenty of online sources for what are called shadow prompts. And these prompts are used to get the ball rolling. You can Google the term 'shadow prompts' and find lists and lists of journal prompts like:

What is a memory you are ashamed of?

When was the last time you self-sabotaged?

Write a letter to the person who's hurt you the most in your life, and tell them everything you'd like to say.

It's heavy stuff, isn't it? And it's something we shouldn't do all at once. This is a process, and I'm sorry to say it's never fully done. It's like exercise, or like learning an instrument, you don't just do it once, or for a week, or for a month, and expect to have it down. It's a practice and a process.

This is a journey of healing and forgiveness, and there are going to be a lot of tears and there are going to be a lot of surprises. When I began incorporating shadow work, I was very surprised how much baggage I was still carrying from my own childhood.

I felt as though, because I seem very settled, and I am very even-tempered, and I am good at making people like me, that meant I managed to make it through 40-something years of some pretty awful shit completely unscathed. But in practice, well, the first time I journaled a shadow prompt I cried. It wasn't even an especially provocative prompt.

The question was simply, what makes you angry? And I had to stop and think. My very first instinct was to hop up on my high horse and simply write that I never get angry. But I felt a little knot in the pit of my stomach and I just had to let the floodgates open. Because that is obviously, *obviously*, untrue. When I was growing up, my defining characteristic was that I was a very good girl. I was calm and well-behaved and polite and helpful and friendly. Because this is how I received approval and recognition and praise.

So while I was staring at this page in my little journal, I had to admit that there are plenty of things that make me angry. There just weren't any ways that I allowed myself to express it. It is incredibly difficult to make myself admit, out loud, to others, when I feel angry, or when I feel wronged, or when I have been hurt. It makes me feel bad, like I am being bad, like people aren't going to like me, that people are going to think I'm high maintenance, or I'm too sensitive, or that I'm not justified in feeling that way, or whatever.

As a result of this shadow, I have throughout my life put up with a lot of bullshit that I shouldn't have. I have allowed people to walk all over me, I have allowed myself to be taken advantage of. Not because I didn't know I was being taken advantage of, but because I couldn't bring myself to say something.

This particular shadow developed as a way to help little Eli behave the way she was expected to so that she wouldn't get in trouble, and so that she could continue to receive the praise that was so important to her.

But this shadow doesn't serve me anymore, and it's time to bring it to the light, recognize and accept why it developed, and understand that denying and suppressing my feelings doesn't actually help me. That was the first prompt I ever did. And it wasn't the hardest one, it should probably have been very easy. But being easy isn't the point. And that is the essence of shadow work.

Art therapy can be another way to kind of work through the feelings and emotions that are kicked up when we begin to do this work. If journaling isn't a method that appeals to you or that works for you, perhaps poetry, or music, singing, drawing, painting, sculpting, dancing, or any other artistic medium will be a better fit. Any way that you can pull those shadows out in front and work through them is going to be crucial to this process.

And we can use magick as well to reinforce this work. Reinforce the work, not instead of the work. As we are confronting our shadows, we may find it helpful to do banishing work, we may need to do a cord cutting, we may want to do candle magic, we might write down certain experiences or shadows and do a ritual burning of those things.

We may find it helpful to carry specific crystals or stones to support us while we work through these issues. We might find it helpful to create an infused oil using specific herbs and plants that we can then anoint ourselves with as another layer of protection and support.

And especially as we begin to identify these generational shadows, it can be very beneficial to call on our ancestors to help us. If we have within our ancestral lineage certain recurring shadows, then it is going to be really healing for not only ourselves, but for the folks who came before us, and the folks who will continue after we are gone. So call them to you and work through these things together.

Performing shadow work is not a quick fix, and it's going to stir up a lot of uncomfortable feelings. It's going to be messy and it's going to seem awful. But what we can expect is an improvement in our emotional wellbeing. Shadow work is crucial for self-forgiveness, and we have to go into it ready to forgive ourselves.

We are going to confront things during this work that we are deeply ashamed of, things that we have done, things we have allowed others to do, maybe things that were forced upon us, and we can't hold judgment against ourselves for any of it. We have to be compassionate and understanding toward ourselves, because the whole point is that we are trying to break these cycles and these patterns.

And that is something we deserve to feel proud of ourselves for. And a side-effect of this work is that it helps us to be more understanding and accepting toward others. Especially when we recognize our shadows in other people. If we have become very cognitively aware of these shadows and how and why they exist in us, we are going to be more sympathetic and empathetic toward others who are harboring those same shadows.

And of course, as an added bonus, we will also begin to see an improvement in our magic. Particularly if we happen to suffer from self-doubt. That little voice in our head when we are performing magick that whispers things like 'this isn't going to work' or 'you're not really a witch' or 'witchcraft is bad' is going to get a lot quieter, and it's going to interfere a lot less.

This is where the real magick comes from, this is where it begins. It begins when we allow ourselves to believe that we are capable of great things. It begins when we accept that we not only deserve to live the life we want, but are capable of creating it.

So mote it be.

MISCELLANEOUS SPELLS, RITUALS, & FORMULAS

What follows here is a mixed bag of spells I've given in various episodes of the podcast. Most of these spells were custom-made in response to different listeners who needed a particular spell for one reason or another.

As with all the spells I ever create, and as with all the advice I ever give, these formulations and rituals are entirely flexible and can be changed as needed. You may want to customize a spell's purpose for your own specific need, you may adjust the ingredients to suit what you have on hand, or you might want to do both.

These are simply blueprints. Keep what works for you, change what doesn't, and as always, write everything down!

Good Sleep Oil

Good sleep oil is really helpful during especially stressful times when the mind won't just let us relax. This oil can be applied before bed to the wrists, the throat, or the temples. We can apply this to candles as well. I prefer to use a vitamin E oil or a sweet almond oil as a carrier because it's meant to be applied to the skin. Into a saucepan, pour 2oz vitamin E or almond oil. Add 1tsp each apple blossoms, peppermint, and thyme for warding nightmares, along with 1tsp each rose petals, chamomile, and lavender for peace. Warm over low heat for 20-30 minutes, strain the herbs, and pour the oil into a small jar or bottle.

←─◇─→

Intuition Moon Water

The New Moon is an especially strong moon phase for intuition, divination, and receiving messages. This moon water is made under the New Moon. Into your jar, add water and a small, clean piece of amethyst, and 1TB dried chamomile. Cover with a lid and place it outside overnight. Strain out the herbs and remove the amethyst in the morning, and use this water in your morning coffee or tea, or as a tribute on your altar.

←─◇─→

Candle Spell For Emotional Healing

This spell is meant to send healing to those who need it. Procure two candles, preferably one white and one green, or they can both be white if that's all you've got on hand. Consecrate the white to represent your target's emotional and spiritual wellbeing. Carve their name or initials into the wax, anoint it with olive oil and sprinkle it with dried rosemary. The green candle represents healing. Focus all of your love for the target into this green candle. Fill it with energies of peace and wellness. Speak a blessing for the target, whatever is in your heart. Speak your intention for this person to be at peace and know that they are safe and loved. Light both candles and let them burn (safely) down.

←⟨⟩→

Strawberry Moon Ritual

The full moon in the month of June is known as the Strawberry Moon. This ritual is meant as an expression of gratitude. For this ritual, we need a couple of fresh summer strawberries. We will also need a candle. A white candle is fine, but you might choose red, orange, yellow, or of course gold. Take a little time to decide on your intention for this full moon. If you don't have something specific to manifest, you can simply express gratitude for all the things that are going well.

Meditate on it for a few moments, then carve your intention into your candle. Take a big bite of your strawberry, and use the bitten side to anoint your candle from the bottom to the top. Focus on imbuing the sweetness of the berry, the freshness, the vitality, into your manifestation or into your expression of gratitude. Then light your candle and allow it to burn down safely, and leave your other strawberry outside as an offering to the birds and the wildlife.

←◇→

Intentional Bonfire Ritual

An excellent way to use fire magick to give a quick jumpstart to your intentions is to burn herbs specific to your needs. For this ritual, you may decide to choose an appropriate moonphase for your bonfire (see the Moon Magick chapter for more information). You may also choose to align your ritual with one of the Celtic fire festivals (Samhain, Imbolc, Beltane, and Lughnasadh).

Observing fire safety, build your fire with intention.

Whether you're alone or with a group, you may play music or drums, you may sing, or even dance around the fire in a clockwise circle in order to raise energy. When the flames are high and you're in the proper mindset, you may choose to throw certain herbs into the fire according to your wishes. Traditional herbs are rosemary or garlic for protection, cinquefoil or basil money manifestation, meadowsweet or lavender for peace, angelica or cedar for healing, rose or willow for love, fern or orange peel for luck, sage or violet to manifest your desires.

Never leave your fire unattended, and make sure to douse it properly and completely at the conclusion of your ritual.

←—◇—→

Psychic Dream Salve

The purpose of this salve is to assist in psychic dream work. To begin with, you'll add ¼ cup of olive oil or vitamin E oil to a small saucepan or a small Crockpot. To the oil, you will add a teaspoon each of any of the following dried herbs, or a combination of yarrow, valerian, peppermint, rosemary, passionflower, mugwort, and chamomile. If you're using a saucepan, allow your herbs to warm on low heat for 20 minutes. If you're using a Crockpot, set them on low for one hour.

Then turn off the heat and strain out the herbs, then return to the pan.

Add a teaspoon or two of beeswax beads to the oil mixture AFTER you've strained out the herbs, but BEFORE it cools completely. Pour your balm into little tins or jars, and let cool until solid. Apply the balm to your third eye before bed to encourage and enhance psychic messages and dreams.

←—◇—→

ACKNOWLEDGEMENT

One doesn't write a book like this in a vacuum. The information in this book is the result of generations of wise women and men, witches, who combined trial and error with what was available to them to create magick.

In addition to the long line of witches who came before me, I must acknowledge the witches around me, who have supported me, encouraged me, and taught me so much. This list includes, but is by no means limited to, Dani, Candice, Fern, Ithil, Jennifer, Kim, and Rhose.

ABOUT THE AUTHOR

Eli Ro

 Eli Ro is a witch, a podcaster, a writer, a tea drinker, and a dog lover. Not necessarily in that order. When she's not spending time in those pursuits, you'll find her with her husband and kids at their home in Southern California.

Listen to her each week on the Middle-Aged Witch Podcast, write to her at eli@middleagedwitch.com, or find her online at middleagedwitch.com.

Made in the USA
Columbia, SC
06 December 2022

72855621R00096